Easy Review™

for

PROPERTY

By

Randy J. Riley, *Esq.*
Seton Hall University Law School

Contributing Editor

Raymond A. Lombardo, *J.D.*
Fordham Law School

Law Rules Publishing Corporation

(800)371-1271

Editorial Staff

Jared S. Kalina, *J.D.*
Cardozo School of Law

Daniel P. Kinsella

Blair C. Pieri

Note: This review publication is not meant to replace required texts as a
substitute or otherwise. This publication should not be quoted from or
cited to. It is meant only to be used as a reminder of some subject matter
and is not a substitute for a comprehensive understanding of the actual
materials which it references or outlines.

Table of Contents

I.   Adverse Possession

A.   In General

1.   Purpose

There are several purposes for adverse possession.
a. To *clear title* to the land.

b. *Reward Land Use*
A factor is that we as a society want land to be
used for development and when that is done for a
specific amount of time we want that to continue.

c. *Expectations*
If someone uses the land for 40 years and makes good
productive use of it, they and the community expect that
the land is theirs.

d. *Bars Claims and Laziness*
This bars someone from sitting on their rights and
watching someone else produce on the land and then
stepping into a reap the benefits.

2.   Four Factors Needed for Adverse Possession
(First: Open, Notorious and Visible; second: Hostile;
third: Continuous; and forth: Period of Time)
The four factors are set by applicable statute of limitation in
the relevant jurisdiction. If statute of limitation is for
example, 21 years, must fulfill all factors for 21 years.

The Four Factors:

a.   Open, Notorious & Visible

(1)   Actual Notice
If the adverse possessor can show that the owner
knew of the possessor's claim to own the land

but did not object (or agree) then the requirement of open, notorious and visible has been met.

(2)   Possessor's Conduct
  (i) Type of Land
      Typically, the more urban the area the requirements of notice are stricter. As you move further into the country and sparse land the less outward notice is necessary.
  (ii) Enclosure
      Using a fence or other barrier puts notice that the land is under control.
  (iii) Actions of Possessor
      Other actions may be:
        (1) Arresting others for trespass;
        (2) Selling part of the land;
        (3) Selling resources off the land;
        (4) Posting of signs.

(3)   Known in the Community
The possessor must make known to all encountered that the land is his own. If the possessor references the land as the true owners then the land cannot be adversely possessed.

b.   Hostile

Adverse to Owner
The possession of land *must be adverse* to the true owners interest. If the owner grants permission for the possessor (licensee or tenant) to be there then the land can never be adversely possessed.

Without Owner's Consent
The possession of the land *cannot occur with the owner' consent*. If the owner actually or

2

constructively consents then the land cannot be adversely possessed.

   (1) **Actual Consent**
The landowner actual states to the possessor that they may use the land.

   (2) **Constructive Consent**
The possessor says to the landowner "I'm going to live on the NE end of your land" and the owner does not respond.

c.   Continuous

   (1) **In General**
The adverse possessor has to hold the property *continuously* to give fair notice that the land is theirs. There are several ways to satisfy the continuous requirement.

   (2) **The continuous requirement:**
Seasonal use of a property is enough to claim adverse possession so long as the seasonal use is continuous.

      (i) **Continuous Seasonal Use**
For example, the possessor seeks to possess a hunting cabin which is used only 2 months of the year. The adverse possession period is 20 years. The possessor must use the cabin for those 2 months every year for 20 years in which to adversely possess.

      (ii) **Whole Year Counted**
If is continuous then the *whole year* is counted toward satisfying the adverse possession time requirements.

(iii) **Designed for Continuous Year Around Use**
There are state by state variations if a structure is designed for continuous year around use. Some states may require that the adverse possessor must be in actual possession for a significant portion of the year for continuity to run.

(3) **Tacking**

(i) **Definition Tacking** = The uniting of the periods of possession of successive adverse possessors to complete the period necessary to establish title by adverse possession, which is possible provided there is *privity* of estate between the successive adverse possessors.
"Tacking is an alternate method of satisfying the limitation period. The original adverse possessor must transfer the property by voluntary conveyance; or inheritance.

(ii) **Continuous Privity**
(Privity = a relationship between parties out of which there arises some mutuality of interest.)
The needs to be continuous vertical privity between the adverse possessors. The previous adverse possessor must pass interest to the subsequent adverse possessor.

(iii) **Example**
An adverse possession statute is for 20 years. Possessor A adversely possesses the land for 15 years continuously. A

sells land to B. B continually possesses the land for 5 years. B is now the owner of the land.

(4) **Termination of Continuous**
Actions of the owner or the possessor may terminate the statute running on the adverse possession.

  (i) **Abandonment**
  If the possessor *abandons* the property then the time period ends. If the possessor returns at a later time then the period starts to run anew. There is no tacking allowed on abandonment.
  For example, A adversely possess land for 10 years. Then, A abandons the property for 6 months. A returns to the property and possesses for 15 years. If the statutory period is 20 years A has not satisfied the time requirements.

  (ii) **Suit by Owner**
  A suit by the owner for trespass or ejectment ends the time period from running *at the filing of the suit*. A temporary reentry is not enough to stop the period. The owner must be trying to permanently remove the possessor from the land.

d. **Period of Time**
A majority of states hold that to adversely possess land, the possessor needs to hold the land for more than 15 years. A substantial majority of those hold it for 20 years to be necessary.

Ownership of Land

Once the statutory period ends the adverse possessor has *superior rights* to the land than the original landowner. However, ownership *does not* automatically transfer. The record holder of the land is still the original landowner. The possessor must bring a Quiet Claim or Declaratory Judgment proceeding in court for the possessor to become the new record owner.

II.   Types of Freehold Estates

A.   Types of Freehold Estates

There are several types of ownership interests in real property.
The term "estate," which refers to an ownership interest comes
from European feudal times, when property interests were
conceptualized in terms of fiefdoms and the like. What the
terminology is really driving at is the absoluteness of the holder's
ownership interest."

1.   Fee Simple

There are different forms that fee simple estate may arise.
Depending on the type of fee simple they are different in
operation, length, creation and termination.

a.   Fee Simple Absolute
(1) Definition:
It is an estate *without restriction* as to
ownership. A fee simple absolute owner holds in
perpetuity as a result.
(2) Creation:
The use of words such as "and his heirs" or "To A
forever." Most states have abolished any magical
language and instead have made it that a fee simple
is assumed unless otherwise noted.
(3) Effect:
This type of freehold is *freely* conveyable,
assignable, transferable and inheritable.
(4) Examples:
"To A"
"To A and his heirs"
"To A and his assigns"

b. **Fee Simple Defeasible**
These are fee simple estates with the potential of infinite duration that can be *terminated by the happening of a specific event*. There are several types of fee simple defeasible:

(1) *Fee Simple Determinable*
  (i) Definition:
      A Fee Simple Determinable is a fee simple estate which ends *automatically* when a stated event occurs.
  (ii) It may prevent the property from being put to a certain use.
  (iii) Unlike the Fee Simple Absolute, the Fee Simple Defeasible has restrictions.
  (iv) The grantor has a *Possibility of Reverter* (see Future Interest chapter III for explanation).
  (v) Adverse Possession (statute) begins to run upon entry when all Adverse Possession conditions are met.
  (vi) Creation:
      To create a Fee Simple Determinable you must use words like "so long as"; "until"; or "during".
  (vii) Example:
      John conveys BonJovi land to Richie so long as BonJovi land is used as a musical hall.
      Note: If condition broken, automatic reversion.

(2) ***Fee Simple Subject to a Condition Subsequent***

    (i)   The Grantor has a ***Right to Re-enter or Entry*** (see Future Interest chapter III for explanation) when a condition occurs.
Example:
Bill conveys Camp David to Newt provided that Camp David remains a weekend resort for White House interns.

    (ii)   Estate ends only when the grantor or her heirs challenge that the condition was breached.

    (iii)   Creation:
To create a Fee Simple Subject to a Condition Subsequent you must use language like "provided that"; "upon express condition"; and "on condition".

    (iv)   Adverse possession begins to run when the grantor or her heirs challenge the action.

(3) ***Fee Simple Subject to an Executory Interest***

    (i)   It is the same as the Fee Simple Determinable and the Fee Simple Subject to a Condition Subsequent except that the right of the land passes to a ***third (3rd) party*** instead of the grantor or her heirs.

    (ii)   Creation:
To create a fee simple subject to an executory interest you must use language like "but if ... then to" or "so long as ... and if not then to".

    (iii)   Adverse possession begins to run upon the occurrence of the event.

    (iv)   Example:
James conveys the Titanic (Titanic is not realty, but assuming a ship is real property) to Leonardo but if the boat is

used for any other purpose than transportation then to Celione and her heirs.

2. Fee Tail

This was an attempt to keep property in the family from *generation to generation indefinitely*. This form of property ownership is no longer valid in the United States. This section will be dealt with briefly.

a. Creation
Use words of limitation such as "to A and the heirs of his body"; "to A and his issue"; or "to A and his children".

b. Modern Interpretation
Words creating a fee tail are now *interpreted* as giving A a life estate (A holds blackacre during his lifetime) and his children a remainder.

3. Life Estate

This is an estate that last for as long as the recipient person is alive. Once the life estate person dies the property goes either to a third person or reverts back to the grantor's lineage.

a. Three Types of Life Estates
(1) *Ordinary Life Estate*
The length of the estate is measured against the *life of the recipient* of the life estate. For example, "to A for life" is a life estate for A for as long as A is alive.

(2) *Per Autre Vie*
The length of the estate is measured against the *life of someone other* that the recipient of the life estate. For example, "to

A for the life of B" is a life estate for A but the measuring time is B's life.

   (3) ***By Operation of Law***
     (i) Fee tail extinction
      In many states, if a fee tail is created, then by law the recipient gets a life estate with a remainder to his heirs.
     (ii) Dower/Curtesy
      A surviving spouse (dower if a widow, curtesy if a widower), the spouse gets a life estate.

b. Powers of a Life Tenant
   (1) Cannot mortgage or sell property.
   (2) Can sell, give or transfer life estate to another.

However, the life estate time is still measure against the original recipient. For example, "to A for life, then to B in fee simple absolute." A may then transfer "to X for life". X may occupy the property for the life of A. A is called the measuring life.

III.   Future Interests

A.   Grantor Future Interests

Future interest in the grantor is termed as *reversionary interests*. There are three types of reversionary interests: possibility of reverter, right of re-entry (entry), and reversion.

1.   Possibility of Reverter
Always associated with *an estate determinable*.

    a.   Based on a Contingent
Possibility of reverter is what the grantor retains if there is a *condition on the use* of the property. For example, X conveys "to A so long as the land is used for school purposes." X has a possibility of reverter. If the condition occurs then the property automatically reverts to X.

    b.   Distinguish from a Reversion
A reversion is an interest in the grantor which is *certain* to occur. For example, X conveys "to A for life", X has a reversion because A is sure to die.

2.   Right of Re-Entry (Entry)
Always associated with *estate subject to a condition subsequent*.

    a.   Based on a Condition
A right of re-entry is retained when a *condition is broken*. For example, Professor X conveys Mansion "to Scott Summers so long as Pepsi is never served on the premises; if Pepsi is sold on the premises Professor X or his heirs may re-enter the premises." If Pepsi is sold on the premises then Professor X has a right, if he chooses to, to re-enter the property and take possession.

    b.   Reversion and Right of Entry
Sometimes a reversion and a right of re-entry is possible. Consider a normal landlord - tenant lease. A landlord at

the end of a lease term has a reversion. However, most leases gives the landlord the right to re-enter the premises if a lease provision is broken. This is a right of re-entry.

3. Reversion

This is a future interest fall back. It springs into being when the estate in the grantee terminates in any other manner than a condition. It reverts back to the grantor. Very similar to the possibility of reverter.

    a. Example
Bill Gates conveys Microsoft "to Ross Perot for life". Bill Gates has a reversion because Ross Perot is sure to pass away and when that happens the estate automatically reverts back to Bill Gates.

    b. No Words of Reversion
It is not necessary to use any words of reversion. All that is necessary is that estate conveyed is *smaller that the original* kept by the grantor. X own fee simple, he transfers a life estate to B. The fee simple estate is greater than the life estate, therefore, reversion.

B. Grantee Future Interest

There are two types of future interests in the grantee: remainder and executory interest (not discussed). Remainders have two sub-categories: contingent and vested. Vested remainders further break down into indefeasibly vested, vested subject to complete divestment, and vested subject to open.

<u>Easy Review Chart Break Down</u>
Remainder
(1) Contingent
(2) Vested
(a) Indefeasibly Vested
(b) Vested Subject to Complete Divestment
(c) Vested Subject to Open

1. Remainder
This is a future interest that comes into being when termination of a prior interest.

    a. Creation
        (1)   Grantor conveys present possessory estate to another.
- "To A for life."

        (2)   Grantor creates a future possessory estate in another ("B") in the same instrument.
- "Upon A's death, to B."

        (3)   The second possessory estate comes into being upon the "natural" termination of the prior estate.
            (i)   No conditions of termination.
            (ii) Life estate
            (iii) Estate for Term of Years

        (4)   Example
Ben & Jerry conveys Ice Cream Land "to Breyer for life, then to Hershey. Ben & Jerry are the grantors. The present interest is in Breyer. Hershey has a remainder upon the death of Breyer.

    b. Distinguished from a Reversion
Remainder vests the estate in someone other than the grantor or his heirs. Reversion causes the estate to revert back to the original grantor or his heirs.

    c. No Remainder after any type of fee simple estate.

2 . **Two Types of Remainders**

    a.   **Contingent Remainder if:**

        (1) *Condition Precedent;*
            (i)   There is a condition that must be met before the remainder becomes possessory.
            (ii)   Example - "to Tommy for life, then if Pamela's living at Tommy's death, to Pamela in fee simple".

        (2) *Remainder in an unborn or unascertained person.*
            Example, to A for life, then to B's children. At the time of execution, B had no children yet. B's unborn children have a contingent remainder. Rule of Perpetuities applies to Contingent Remainder.

    b.   **Vested Remainders**

        (1) *Indefeasibly Vested*
            This is a future interest in which is *certain* to become possessory. For example, Grant conveys Virginia "to Lee for life , remainder to Lincoln and his heirs". Lincoln has a vested remainder.

        (2) *Vested Subject to Complete Divestment*
            This is a future interest which *may vest if a prior possessory interest terminates in time*. For example, Mickey conveys Disney "to Goofy for life, then to Donald for life." Goofy has a life estate, but Donald has a vested remainder subject to complete divestment. Donald only gets Disney if he outlives Goofy. If Donald dies before Goofy he has nothing and Disney reverts to Mickey and his heirs upon Goofy's death.

(3) ***Vested Remainder Subject To Open***
This is a future interest which is *certain to vest in some but there remains a chance that others who are not ascertained may share* in the estate. This is common with children when additional children may be born. For example, JFK conveys Massachusetts to "Rose for life, remainder to Ted's children". At the time of conveyance Ted only has one child B. B has a vested remainder subject to open. But Ted is still alive to have other children and B could have to share with other children subsequently born. The class closes upon the death of Ted. At Ted's death, whoever his children are become vested remainders.

C.   Conveyance Rules and Doctrines

1.   No Gap in Seisin
There can be no gap in conveyance. If there is a gap then it reverts back to the grantor. For example, A conveys Blackacre "to B for life." After B dies there is a gap. A automatically retains a reversion to preserve continuity in ownership.

2.   Merger Rule
A merger takes place when a person hold *two successive possessory estates*. For example, Daffy conveys Loony Toons "to Bugs for life, then to Bugs." Bugs gets the estate immediately as a fee simple estate. There are two times merger does not work:

a.   Fee Tail
A fee tail cannot merge with a fee simple. But as previously stated, fee tails are no longer part of estate planning in the United States.

b.   Interrupted Vested Remainders
Two vested interests don not merge if there is an intervening contingent remainder.

17

3. Doctrine of Worthier Title

If a grantor attempts to convey property with a future interest going to the grantor's heirs then the future interest turns into a reversion. For example, Willie Wonka conveys Chocolate Factory "to the Umpalumpa's for life, and then to the heirs of Willie Wonka." Umpalumpa gets a life estate and Willie Wonka retains a reversion.

4. Rule in Shelly's Case

If a transfer gives a freehold estate to a person and the remainder in that same persons heirs, the transfer is deemed a fee simple transfer. For example, Aquaman transfers Atlantis "to Superman for life, remainder in Superman's heirs." Superman takes the property as a fee simple.

5. Rule Against Perpetuities

An interest must vest within 21 years of some life in being at the creation of the interest of the conveyance or it fails. The four elements are:

a. Vesting Element

Applies to contingent remainders and executory interests. A contingent remainder vests when the grantee is ascertainable and there are no further conditions precedent. An executory interest vests when they receive possession.

b. Does Not Have to Vest

It is not necessary for the interest to actually vest. The rule is designed so that vesting would not occur to far in future.

c. 21 Year Rule

The rule does not allow for conveyance to occur more than 21 years after a life in being.

d. Life in Being

The measuring life must be found in the conveyance. It does not have to be the grantor it can be another.

IV. Concurrent Ownership of Property

A. In General

There are three (3) types of concurrent ownership of property: joint tenant, tenants-in-common, and the tenancy by the entireties. Each carry distinct characteristics.

B. Joint Tenancy

1. Definition
This is a form of co-ownership in which the tenant owners *own an undivided interest* in the whole estates.

a. Full Owner with Rights
Each joint tenant has a right to possess or occupy the *whole* entire property. Every tenant shares the exact same right in the property.

b. Right of Survivorship
This is the most significant factor in joint tenancy. Upon the death of one joint tenant the remaining interest *automatically* goes to the surviving tenants. A joint tenancy interest cannot be passed to heirs.

2. Creation
The law has held that to create a joint tenancy there need to be *four "unities"* at the time of the creation. If one is lacking then a tenancy-in-common is created instead of the joint tenancy.

a. Unity of Interest
All of the tenants must share the exact same interest in the property as to share and duration.

b. Unity of Time
All of the tenants interest in the property must vest at the same time.

c.   **Unity of Possession**
As stated before, all the tenants must have a right to occupy the entire premises.

d.   **Unity of Title**
This simple means that all the tenants acquired their interest by the same instrument, usually by will or deed.

3.   **Words to Create**
a.   At common law, there is a presumption that any transfer such as "to A and B" is automatically a joint tenancy (note that many states by statute have overruled this). Other words are "to A and B jointly," "to A and B together," and "to A and B as joint tenants."
b.   At common law, a person cannot create a joint tenancy by transferring property they own to themselves and another. For example, A transfers Blackacre "to A and B as joint tenants" is not allowed. However, many states have allowed this type of transfer by statute.

4.   **Termination**

Joint tenancies can be terminated very easily during the life of the joint tenants.

a.   **Inter Vivos Transfer**
If a joint tenant transfers her interest in the property during her life then the joint tenancy is severed.
(1) The joint tenancy will become a tenancy-in-common.
(2) The interest in the property being split equally among the tenants.

b.   **Mortgage**
(1) Majority of states, a mortgage is not a transfer of interest or title and therefore does not in itself terminate a joint tenancy. However, if foreclosure occurs then that does terminate the joint tenancy.

(2) Minority of states hold to a title theory of mortgages where a mortgage is a transfer of title. Therefore, a mortgage automatically terminates a joint tenancy.

c   Partition Suit
A tenant may sue in court for the court to order that the land be separated. In that case, the court splits the land with each tenant receiving a fee simple interest in their divided section.

d   Leases
Leases do not destroy a joint tenancy. In essence, the court held that a lease is not a conveyance of permanent interest in land.

C.   Tenancy -In-Common

1.   Definition
This is where the tenants own an undivided, separate and distinct share of the property.

a.   No Right to Survivorship
Unlike in joint tenancy there is not right to survivorship.

b.   Varying Ownership Interest
Tenants may own varying amount of shares (i.e., Eddie owns 10%, Alex owns 30%, and David owns 60%).

c.   Freely Alienable
A tenant may pass their interest in the property by inheritance, sale, gift, or any other transfer.

2. **Creation**
Modern statutes hold the tenancy-in-common as the default
ownership rights.

    a. **Termination of Joint Tenancy**
See, e.g., D'Ercole, 407 F.Supp. 1377, 1380 (death of all
joint tenants terminates.

    b. **Termination of Tenancy By the Entireties**
See U.S. v. Jacobs, 111 NY, 306 US 363 (dissolution of
marriage terminates).
Essentially same as joint tenancy but for fact feudal
property law regarded husband and wife as one person.

    c. **Default**
Failure to meet any of the requisites of a joint tenancy or
tenancy by the entireties defaults to a tenancy in common.

    d. **Words to Create**
A joint tenancy can be created by "to A and B" if you are in
a state with default statute provisions, "to A and B as joint
tenants," or "to A for 10% and B for 90% of ownership."

3. **Termination**

    a. **Ouster**
If one tenant ousts the other tenant from possessory interest
in the property. The ousted person can sue to re-gain
possessory interest but they cannot oust the other.

    b. **Transfer of property**
The tenancy in common continues but with a new tenant.

D.   **Tenancy By the Entireties**
This is a co-ownership similar to the joint tenancy but based solely on husband and wife ownership.

1.   **Definition**
At common law the husband and wife are regarded as one person in respects of ownership of property. Each spouse owns the entire property with rights to use and occupation.

a.   **Right of Survivorship**
Just like the joint tenancy the tenancy by the entireties enjoys a right of survivorship.

2.   **Creation**
Almost like the joint tenancy, the tenancy by the entireties require five (5) "unities."

a.   **Unity of Time**
Same as joint tenancy.

b.   **Unity of Interest**
Same as joint tenancy.

c.   **Unity of Possession**
Same as joint tenancy.

d.   **Unity of Title**
Same as joint tenancy.

e.   **Unity of Person**
For there to be a tenancy by the entireties there must be a lawful marriage. Common law marriage is sufficient to create a tenancy by the entireties.

f.   **Words to Create**
Regardless of any language used, any transfer to a husband and wife is deemed as a tenancy by the entireties, even if other tenancy language is used. For example, A and B are

husband and wife. X transfers Blackacre "A and B as joint tenants." Blackacre is actually owned by A and B as tenants by the entireties.

3.   **Termination**

    a.   Transfer
    Both the husband and wife must join in their conveyance of the property for the transfer to terminate the tenancy. If only one spouse attempts to transfer the property then the transfer is invalid.

    b.   Death of a Spouse
    Death of a spouse changes the property into a fee simple ownership for the surviving spouse.

    c.   Divorce
    Divorce, and by court order, severs the tenancy by the entireties. Either the court will award the property to one person or the divorce creates a tenancy in common.

    d.   Joint Creditor
    A joint creditor can reach and seize tenancy by the entireties property. However, if one spouse is not a debtor then the creditor cannot seize the property.
       (1)   Death of the Debtor Spouse
           The creditor *losses all interest* in the property until the death of the other spouse.
       (2)   Death of the Non-Debtor Spouse
           The Creditor *may seize* the property because the debtor spouse is now the fee simple owner of the property.

V.   Other Ownership Interests and Their Creation

A.   **Tenancy for Years**

    1.   **Definition** - an estate that lasts for *some fixed period of time* or for a time computable by a formula that results in fixing calendar dates for beginning and ending.

        a.   **Tenancy of no fixed period terminable upon some event.**
Date computable for ending is computable upon the happening of some event (i.e., O rents to A "for the duration of the war.")

        b.   **Term of years determinable** -
A term of years terminable upon some event or subject to condition subsequent (i.e., O rents to A for five years "so long as it is used as a factory.")

        c.   **Day of beginning and ending** -
Unless the parties specify otherwise, a lease begins on the earliest moment of the beginning day and ends before midnight on the last day.

    2.   **No maximum permitted term** (unless statutorily restricted).

    3.   **Termination of tenancy for years**
Term of years expires at the end of the stated period *without either party giving notice.*

B.   **Periodic Tenancy**

    1.   **Definition** - tenancy for a period of some fixed duration that continues for succeeding periods *until either* the landlord or the tenant gives notice of termination. If NO notice is given the tenancy is automatically extended for another period.

Note: All extensions are part of the same tenancy → meaning all the same conditions apply unless noted otherwise.

2. **Creation of Periodic Tenancies**

   a. **Creation by express agreement of the parties**
   L and T may expressly create an estate that is to extend from period to period (i.e., "L to T for one year, and at the end of that term, the lease shall continue in effect from month to month, unless ended by written notice.")

   b. **Creation by agreement only as to rent period**
   Often provision is made for payment of rent monthly with no set termination. The periodic tenancy is measured by the rental periods.

      (1) **Annual rent payable monthly situations**
      If an annual rent is specified, the estate is from year to year, even though rent is to be paid in monthly installments. Monthly payments are viewed as merely to the convenience of the parties. The minority view is that it creates a month-to-month tenancy.

      (2) **Significance**
      If the lease is from year to year, six (6) months notice is required for termination. If T holds over for any period of time, L can hold T liable for another years rent. If month to month, either L or T can terminate with a month's notice.

   c. **Creation by operation of law**

      (1) **Where a T holds over after expiration of the term**
      If T holds over, L may elect to consent to T's staying over and hold T liable for any additional term.

      (2) **Where T takes possession under an invalid lease**
      Mere entry into possession by T creates a *tenancy at will*. However, the payment of rent converts

the tenancy at will into a tenancy from period to period.

3. **Requirement of Notice of Termination**
Most distinctive feature → continues until proper notice is given. Notice can be given orally or written.

    a. **Common Law Rules**
        (1)   **How much notice?**
            Notice must be equal to the length of the rental period itself, except in an annual lease (6 months).
        (2)   **Notice must specify the last period day.**
            Notice must fix last period day of period as the date of termination and not intervening date (i.e., month to month lease beginning the 1st; if notice is given on February 20th that is not sufficient to terminate on March 20th→ the actual termination day is the last day of March).
        (3)   **When notice must be given?**
            Notice must be given so that T or L will receive the required amount of notice prior to the expiration of the current term (i.e., year to year beginning on January 1st; notice must be given prior to July 1st in order to terminate on December 31st of that year).

C. **Tenancy at Will**

1. **Definition** - is a tenancy of no stated duration that endures only so long as both L and T desire. *Either party can terminate at any time.* Tenancy at will can arise expressly, or more likely, by operation of law when the intended tenancy fails for some reason.

    a. **Tenant's possessory rights -**
        A tenant at will is not merely a licensee because he has an *estate in land*. Therefore, tenant has *possession*. (*See*

27

licensee discussion *infra*.) The significance is that T can maintain a trespass action against a 3rd party or the L.

b. **Tenancy terminable by only one party**
A leasehold that is terminable at will by *only one party* is not a tenancy at will. (Must go both ways). The first step in determining what estate is created is to ask if only one party can terminate ascertain whether or not the power to terminate is affixed to a term of years or periodic tenancy.
   (1) Lease for certain duration terminable by one party - If termination provision is for a term of years or a periodic tenancy, the lease creates a determinable tenancy, not a tenancy at will.
   (2) Lease of no certain duration - If no duration and one party has power to terminate the courts are split between tenancy at will and determinable life estate.

2. **Termination**

   a. **Termination by acts of the parties** -
   If either party manifests an intention that the estate come to an end, this terminates the tenancy at will. The L usually gives a notice to quit, whereas the T abandons the premise or gives notice.
      (1) **Notice not required at common law**
      Neither party had to give notice for a period of time as a prerequisite to terminating a tenancy at will. Tenancy terminates the day notice is received.
      (2) **Statutes usually require notice**
      Most states have statutory notice period = usually 30 days.

   b. **Termination by operation of law** -
   NO ASSIGNMENT ALLOWED
   Sale of property by L or even *attempt* terminates the tenancy. Death of either party terminates the tenancy.

D. **Statute of Frauds**

1. **Short Term Lease Exception**

   Most states have no written requirement for leases of *less than one (1) year*. An oral lease for more than one year creates a tenancy at will.
   Note: If a state has no short term exception → an oral lease creates a tenancy at will.

2. **Oral Lease to Commence in the Future**
   The courts measure the one year short term lease *from the time occupancy starts*. Therefore, a majority of courts hold that a lease to commence in the future is valid if the term does not exceed one (1) year.

3. **Option to Renew Oral Lease**
   Where oral lease is renewable at the option of the lessee, the lease is usually held as extending to the end of the option period. Thus, if the oral lease is for one (1) year term, with an option to renew for another year, the lease is treated as a two (2) year lease and is void if the short term exception is one (1) year.

4. **Entry and Paying Rent Under an Invalid Lease**
   Although an oral lease not complying with the Statute of Frauds is void, entry by a T under an oral lease creates a tenancy at will. As soon as T pays rent, a periodic tenancy is created. However, there is some difference of opinion as to what the period of tenancy is:

   a. **Year-to-Year**: Majority view is that a year to year tenancy is created regardless of how the rent is paid. The rationale being that since the invalid lease was necessarily for term exceeding one (1) year, a year-to-year tenancy comes the closest to approximating the parties' intentions.

   b. **Rent Calculation**: Determined by how the rent is to be paid in invalid lease (i.e., if rent is calculated on an annual basis, even though payable monthly, a year-to-year tenancy created).

29

    c. **Rent Payment:** Determine period by way rent is actually paid NOT how it is calculated.

E. **Tenancy at sufferance (Holdover Tenant)**

When a tenant holds over after termination of tenancy he is called a tenant at sufferance. Not a tenant (because is there without permission) or a trespasser (Because the original possession was not wrongful).

Landlord's Choices:
(1) Consent
    a. Express
    b. Implied - L is silent but takes rent.
(2) Eviction

---

1. **Rationale**
Eviction as a deterrent to holding over. Holding over is frowned upon because new tenants should be able to move in promptly upon the expiration of a prior tenancy.

2. **Length of New Term**
In most jurisdictions, holding over gives rise to a periodic tenancy. Period can be measured by:
a. **Way rent is reserved in the original lease;**
b. **Length of the original term.**
Note: Maximum length is limited to one year.

3. **Provisions of the New Term**
New tenancy is usually governed by the provisions in the old lease, including provisions for the payment of rent. If L notifies T he must pay higher rent for holdover → he will be liable unless he notifies L that he refuses to pay.

4. **Self-Help in Recovering Possession**
Most states require that L rely on the judicial process for eviction. However, many courts allow L to use self-help to evict a T holding over period for **no more force than is necessary**.

VI. Landlord's Duty Not to Discriminate

A. Civil Rights Act of 1866

Provides: "All citizens of the U.S. shall have the same right, in every State and Territory, as is enjoyed by white citizens thereof to inherit, purchase, lease, sell, hold, and convey real and personal property."

1. **Bars racial or ethnic discrimination only**
Forbids discrimination against blacks and any identifiable minority group "intentionally discriminated against" because of their ancestry or ethnic characteristics as opposed to place of origin or religion.

2. **Applies to all property transfers**
Applies to sale or rental of all property, not just to housing.

3. **Remedies**
Remedies under this Act are an injunction against the L or seller; and/or damages.

B. Fair Housing Act of 1968

Makes it unlawful to refuse to sell or rent a *dwelling* to any person because of race, color, religion or national origin (amended later to include gender). In 1988, amended to include discrimination against:
(1) Person with children except in bona fide senior citizen housing;
(2) Handicaps/Disabilities (does not include drug addicts or alcoholics).

1. **Advertising**
Prohibits making any public statement that indicates a discriminating preference.

2. **Exemptions**
Provides that dwellings for private clubs, religious organizations, and certain specified persons are exempt from the act.

    a. **Single Family Dwellings**: A person leasing or selling a dwelling she owns is exempt if she:
        (1) Does not own more than three such dwellings;
        (2) Does not use a broker;
        (3) Does not advertise in a manner that discriminates.

    b. **Small owner-occupied multiple unit**: Must be a builder of four (4) units or less, and she occupies one of the units and does not discriminatorily advertise.

3. **Enforcement**
Aggrieved persons may sue the seller in federal court without regard to usual jurisdictional requirements. Courts may award an injunction, actual damages, and punitive damages.

C. **Proving Discrimination**

1. **Prima facie case - Discriminatory Effects**
Proof of discriminatory effects is sufficient to make out a prima facie case that the Fair Housing Act or Section 42 USC1982 is violated. **Proof of discriminatory INTENT is NOT necessary.**

2. **Shift of Burden of Proof**
Once the plaintiff establishes a prima facie case the burden of proof shifts to the defendant to come forward with evidence to show that her actions were not motivated by considerations of race.

VII. Landlord's Duty to Deliver Possession

A. Legal Right to Possession

L has the duty of transferring to the T at the beginning the *legal right* to possession. If another person has *paramount title* and is legally entitled to possession → L is in default and liable.

1. Paramount Title
Refers to any title or interest in the leased land held by a 3rd party at the time the lease is made, that is paramount to the interest of L (i.e., L gives M a mortgage on property P, M records mortgage, M has paramount title).

2. Tenant's Remedies Prior to Entry
T may *terminate the lease* if there was paramount title that he didn't know about when he signed the lease. However, if T *knows of the paramount title when signing the lease*, T is presumed to *waive* the possibility of eviction. Note: makes it important for L to disclose all relevant information.

3. After the tenant Enters into Possession
Once in possession, T has *no remedy* unless he is actually evicted by paramount title. Possession shows a presumption that he has accepted L's title as adequate for his use of the property.

B. **Actual Possession**

1. **English Rule: Majority View**
   L has to *deliver actual possession* to T, as well as right to possession, at the beginning of the term. L is in default if previous T has not moved out or he does not remove previous T within a reasonable period of time.

   a. **Rationale**
   Carries out intentions of the parties since the T bargains for *use of property* rather than a lawsuit against the prior T. Also, L *has more knowledge* as to whether or not the previous T is moving out or staying. Finally, L is more *familiar with eviction procedures*.

   b. **Tenant's Remedies**
   (1) Terminate lease and recover damages for finding another place (storage rental, motel, phone calls, gas);
   (2) Affirm lease, refuse to pay for rent during time wasn't occupying and recover damages for time unable to occupy.

   c. **Part Possession**
   New T is entitled to abatement in rent and damages if prior T holds over only part of the property and T takes possession of the other part.

2. **American Rule: Minority View**
   L has *no duty* to deliver actual possession at commencement of the term and is not in default when previous T continues to wrongfully occupy the premises.

   a. **Rationale**
   (1) Only a leasehold $\rightarrow$ up to T to take possession if he wants it;
   (2) T has right to evict the holdover by summary proceeding;
   (3) L should not be liable for tortuous acts of holdover T;

34

(4) L is not required to evict a trespasser after T takes possession, therefore, he shouldn't have to before T takes possession.

b.   Remedies against the holdover T
   a. Sue to evict the holdover and recover damages;
   b. T can treat holdover T as a holdover for another term and collect rent himself.

VIII. Landlord's Duty Not to Interfere with Quiet Enjoyment of the Property

A. **Covenant of Quiet Enjoyment**
Quiet enjoyment defined - T will enjoy possession and use of premises/property in piece and without disturbance. Protects T's right to be free of meddlesome interference with his or her tenancy.
Always implicit in every lease, L may not interfere with T's *quiet enjoyment* of the leased premises.

1. **Dependent Covenant**
T's covenant to pay rent is dependent on L's performance of his covenant of quiet enjoyment. Even at common law this was an exception to the rule that covenants were independent.

2. **Breach**
Can breach by either actual or constructive eviction. No rent would be due, just a release from the lease at the time of the breach.

B. **Actual Eviction**
If T is evicted from the entire leased property – either by L or by someone with paramount title – T's rental obligations cease immediately. Any liability for future rents are extinguished.

1. **Partial Eviction by L**
T's rental obligation abates entirely until possession of the whole is restored. T may remain in possession and refuse to pay rent.

2. **Partial Eviction by Paramount Title**
If T sues as contemplated by parties is interfered with by one with paramount title, T may terminate the lease, receive damages, or receive a partial abatement. If T continues in possession, he remains liable for the reasonable value of the portion he possesses.

C. **Constructive Eviction**

Where through the fault of the L, there occurs a substantial interference with the T's use and enjoyment of the leased premises, so that the T can no longer enjoy the premises as the parties contemplated. The T may terminate the lease, vacate the premises, and be excused from further rent liability. T has to move out in a timely basis from the occurrence of the L act. Can not remain in the premises.

1. **Elements of Constructive Eviction**

a. **Substantial Interference:** measured *objectively* → it is what a reasonable person would regard as fundamentally incompatible with the use and enjoyment for which the parties bargained. Courts consider:
- Purpose for which the property was leased;
- Forseeability of the interference;
- Duration of the interference;
- Nature and degree of harm caused;
- Availability of means to abate the interference.

(1) **Disclosure Prior to Lease**: If L knows of defects in the premises he may be under a duty to disclose these to the T.

(2) **T's knowledge**: If T knows of the interference prior to taking possession, and subsequently takes possession, T has waived the interference.

(3) **Notice to L:** Prior to claiming constructive eviction → T must give notice to L of the objectionable conduct and L must fail to remedy the situation in a reasonable period.

b.   Abandonment
T cannot claim constructive eviction unless and until he vacates the premises. He cannot remain in possession and refuse to pay rent or receive damages under this doctrine. If T stays → obligation of rent continues.

(1) **Declaratory Judgment**: may be available to T to determine whether he would be justified in vacating.

(2) **Damages after Vacating**: once T vacates, the lease is terminated. T can recover damages.

(3) **Vacating within a Reasonable Period**: to claim, T must vacate within a reasonable period after L's acts to justify the vacation. If T does not, he has waived L's breach.

(4) **Restatement View**: does not require vacation of premises. Does treatment parallel actual eviction?

c.   Fault of the Landlord
Interference must result from some or failure to act by L. Generally, this is not available when the interference has resulted from acts of *3rd parties*.

(1) **Annoyance caused by other T**: L is not responsible. Must call police or action in court directly against other T.
Exception: If L causes a condition (i.e., renting to another T) that he knows will interfere with another T he is responsible.
For example: L has building with T1 is a library. then rents space to T2, in same building, who intends to use as a disco.

(2) **Nuisance**: L has a duty not to permit a nuisance on the premise.

(3) **Common areas**: duty to control acts and problems in common areas (i.e., shared stairwell, shared walkways).

2.   Modern Trend
L is responsible if legal action can be taken against 3rd parties.

IX. Landlord's Duty to Provide Habitable Premises

A. Landlord's Duty at the Inception of the Lease

1. Common Law
There is no implied covenant by L that the premises are tenantable condition or are fit for purposes intended. *Caveat emptor (lessee): T must inspect the premises and protect himself.*
Note: *Taken as is!*
Rationale: Common Law favored Landlord's over serf-T's

a. Exceptions
(1) **Furnished home for a short term**
Short term leases for a furnished home (i.e., summer house) has as implied covenant that premises are tenantable. Rationale: No time to inspect the premises.
(2) **Hidden (latent) defects**
When known to L and not easily discoverable →
L has a duty to disclose the defect (i.e., terminates where damages can not be seen, weakened stairs).
(3) **Building under construction**
If building is being built for a specific purpose and lease is executed before building finished → implied covenant for that use.

b. Independent Covenants Rule
Independent covenants rule is defined as an obligation to pay independently not contingent upon L delivering the premises in habitable condition.
Even if there is an express warranty the T must overcome the independent covenants rule if T wants to terminate the lease or be excused from rent. Under the rule, T is not excused from performance by L's breach → T's remedy is to sue L.

2. Implied covenant of habitability
In recent years courts have held that there is an implied warranty in *urban dwellings*, such as apartments. They have further held that T is relieved of responsibilities when L breaches the implied covenant.

a. Restatement View
Implies a covenant of *suitability* if "the parties contemplate that the leased property will be used for residential purposes" and if the non-suitable condition is not the fault of T. Not a standard of *perfection BUT* on of *bare minimal standards*.

b. Rationale
  (1) Modern urban T doesn't have time to inspect the premise.
  (2) L knows more about defects and is in better position to remedy them.
  (3) Housing codes, imposes duties onto L.
  (4) Because of housing shortage → T's have much less bargaining power.
  (5) UCC implies covenant for sale of goods.

c. Scope of Warranty
Premises are fit for habitation at time of letting.
Scope of *initial warranty* of habitability doesn't receive as much attention as *continuing duty of habitability*.
  (1) **Latent defects only**
        L might only have a duty for latent defects → IF T KNOWS of the defect he will have *waived his claim* if he still sign the lease.

  (2) **Housing Code**
        Establishes an implied convenant of habitability. Most Courts hold that a substantial violation of the local housing code is a violation of the *implied covenant of habitability*. The continuing duty of

habitability imposed on L is a result of the implied covenant of habitability.

d. Remedies for a Breach
Remedies for a breach of covenant of habitability include:
(1) Move out and terminate the lease;
(2) Repair and deduct the cost from the rent;
(3) Reduce rent to fair value;
(4) Stay and pay full rent while suing the L.

e. Waiver by tenant (residential only)
T can waive *minor defects BUT* it is against public policy to allow T to waive *major defects which render the premises unsafe.*
Restatement View: Forbids waiver of even small defects when: (1) defect renders premises unsafe; or (2) waiver is unconscionable or against public policy.

B   Landlord's Duty to Repair After Entry by Tenant

1. Common Law
L has *no duty* to maintain and repair the premises. Came about because early all lands were agricultural and possession of land was the important thing. The buildings were incidental to the primary purpose of the lease.
Landlord's covenant to repair
Parties can by agreement put the duty to repair on the L. However, L's covenant to repair is always *independent* of T's covenant to pay rent. This breach does *not excuse* T from payment of rents.

2. Restatement View
Provides for an implied covenant of *suitability* continuing for the duration of the lease. Covenant is breached if L fails to repair defects within a reasonable period of time.
Note: *Rationale is same as implying for habitability.*

43

3. **Scope of the Warranty**
   Courts differ on what standards used to measure L's duty.
   a. **Housing Code**: Violations of housing code is a violation of the covenant.

   b. **Fit for Human Habitation**: Standard may be higher or lower than the housing code requirements.

   c. **Notice to the Landlord**: Most courts state that L has a *reasonable period* to repair after notice is given.

4. **Remedies for Breach - Modern View**
   T's covenant to pay rent is dependent on L's performance under the implied warranty of habitability.

   a. **Terminate Lease**
      T may terminate lease, vacate the premises, and recover damages. Damages may include relocation costs and fair market value of the lease.

   b. **Continue Lease and Recover Damages**
      T may continue lease and recover damages in rent reduction. The court may calculate by (1) pay for premises as is or (2) the fair value between the premise as is now and the way it should be. Generally no more than 15% - 20% reduction.

   c. **Continue Lease and Use Rent to Repair**
      T may use a reasonable amount of rent to repair the defective condition.

   d. **Continue Lease and Withhold Rent**
      T may, after notice to L, place his rent in escrow until fault is determined. T can not just not pay rent, the rent must be paid to escrow.

   e. **May use L's breach** of the *continuing duty of maintaining premises* as a Defense in L's Rent Action.

5. **Waiver by Tenant**
   A waiver of L's obligations under implied covenant of habitability is not permitted because public policy to give T's power to enforce housing codes.

   a. **URLTA View**
      Lease can shift duty to repair to T if:
      (1) Agreement is not for purposes of evading obligations of L and is placed in a separate writing;
      (2) Work is not necessary to cure non-compliance with housing code.
      •*Housing Code always comes first.*

   b. **Restatement View**
      Parties may agree to decrease L's obligations unless agreement is *unconscionable* or *against public policy*.

   c. **Statutory Duties of Landlord**
      Many states lay out the duty and tell whether or not can be waived by the T.

   d. **Retaliatory Eviction**
      If T reports L for violation of the housing code, L may try to evict T or refuse to renew lease. Most of the retaliatory evictions result from T complaining about a violation of a housing code. This is illegal. The L may be sued for injunction and damages.
      • If eviction is tried 3-6 months after T reports L, in many states, then it is *presumed that eviction is on the account of the reporting*. This is state by state issue.

X . Landlord's Tort Liability

A. Dangerous Condition Existing at Time of Lease
Caveat emptor (lessee) is the common law rule. L is not liable for injuries to T or T's guests due to a dangerous condition of the premises.

Note: The following **Exceptions**:
1. **Concealed dangerous conditions (latent defects)**
   L has a duty to disclose dangerous conditions which he knows of and knows T will not realize the risk. L is liable for any injuries resulting from this condition.
   Rationale: If L discloses it then T can minimize the risk by remedying it.
   Note: *There is no liability after disclosure to the T.*

2. **Public Use**
   a. If lease contemplates that premises will be sued as place of public admission → L is liable if:
      (1) Knows or should know of the condition;
      (2) Has reason to expect T will not correct before admitting the public;
      (3) Fails to exercise reasonable care to remedy the condition.
      Liability only extends to those who enter for public purposes.
   b. Defects must exist at the beginning of the lease.
   c. Tenant's promise to repair
      If T promises to repair the defect → L is still liable if reason to expect that T will admit public before repairing.

3. **Defects arising after Tenant Takes Possession**
   General rule is that L has no liability for personal injury from dangerous conditions that *arise after* T takes possession. Duty to care for the premises is incumbent on the T.

Exception: Repairs Undertaken
Once L voluntarily undertakes to make repairs she is
under a *duty to exercise reasonable care*. L is
liable if injury results from negligent repair.

4. **Common Areas Controlled by Landlord**
If L maintains any control of common areas → liable for
injuries if L could have reasonably discovered the
condition and made it safe.
Note: *L may be liable for criminal intruders if it is
foreseeable.*

5. **Landlord May Have Contracts to Repair**

6. **Landlord may have statutory duty to repair.**

7. **Exculpatory Clause**
Clauses which relieve L of all or part negligent or shared
liability for injuries resulting from L's negligence are
enforced by few courts. Less likely to be enforced in
residential settings because of the lack of bargaining
power.

XI. Tenant's Duties

A. Duty to Pay Rent

Duty to pay rent is an *independent obligation at common law*. Modern trend is towards K law, and away from property law. state by state inquiry. The duty to pay rent is not dependent upon L's performance of her obligations. In many jurisdictions, T's duty to pay rent is dependent on L's performance of obligations only if the premises is a *residential* one.

1. **Implied Agreement**
    If rent is not reserved, T has a duty to pay the *reasonable rental value* of the property.

2. **Illegal Agreement**
    If the rental agreement is illegal because the housing code forbids renting property in sub-standard condition, T has no duty to pay rent. But T must pay the reasonable rental value of the premises.

3. **Rent Passes with Reversion**
    The right to rent is attached to L's reversion. If L sells the property to another, the transferee is entitled to future rents.

4. **Non-apportionment of Rent**
    In absence of an agreement to the contrary, rent falls due on the *last day of the lease term*.

5. **Rent Control**

    a. **Constitutionality**
        Regulating rents has been held constitutional on the theory that it bears a rational relation to a legitimate public purpose, the welfare of housing consumers.

b.   Reasonable Return
Rental control ordinances must provide L with a just and reasonable return or they are an unconstitutional taking.

c.   Eviction of Tenant
Under rent control ordinances, L cannot evict a T at the end of a term and rent to a new T at the market rate. Must be renewal of lease unless there is *good cause* to evict.

B.   Duty to Repair

Common Law Duty
Absent a duty on part of L, T has a duty to make ordinary repairs to keep the property in the same condition as at the commencement of the term. T *does not have a duty* to make substantial repairs but must prevent damage.

1.   Tort Liability
If T has a duty to repair, T is liable to persons injured as a result of his failure to repair.

2.   Covenant by Tenant to Repair
If T covenants → liable for repairs whatever the cause. Even if property is totally destroyed. Need to get renter's insurance. This is in almost every residential lease.

3.   Repair and Deduct View
T has responsibility to repair anything within their power/ability to repair and then deduct the reasonable costs from the rent.

C. Duty not to Damage the Premises

If T substantially damages the premises by an affirmative act, T is liable to L. This is known as *voluntary* or *affirmative* *waste*.

1. Changes in the Premises
But: Must generally post a bond to ensure that the work is finished (presuming it is allowed).
Modern trend - long term T may change a structure if the economic value is not diminished.

2. Restatements View
T is entitled to make changes in the physical condition of the leased property which are *reasonably necessary* in order for T to use premises in a reasonable manner.

D. Duty not to Disturb Other Tenants
Only a duty not to commit a nuisance. Many residential apartment leases provide a covenant by the T that he will not substantially interfere with the use or enjoyment of other tenants with their properties.

E. Duty not to Use for Illegal Purposes
T has a duty not to use premises for an illegal purpose.
L's remedies depend upon their complicity in the legal use.

1. Landlord Intends Illegal Use:
If L and T both intend that property be used for an illegal purpose, the lease is *not enforceable* by either party.

2. Landlord not a Party to Illegality
If T uses premises for an illegal purpose not intended by L → L cannot terminate the lease and can only seek an injunction of the activities (unless a nuisance to other tenants - then can seek eviction).

F. **Acts of Third (3rd) Parties Relieving Tenant of Duties**
T may be relieved of his duty to pay rent by acts of 3rd parties that make it impossible or difficult to continue the lease. However, must start with the proposition that T has purchased a term and *assumed the risk* (so long as the L did not forseeably create the situate).

1. **Use Becomes Illegal**
Where third party (other than government action, which usually makes use illegal) causes use of property to become illegal after the lease is made, a court may hold that the T1 may terminate the lease and stop paying further rent. The L and T1 both know the intended use of property.

2. **Frustration of Purpose**
T may terminate the lease in case of extreme hardship if the purpose of the lease is frustrated. Most frequently frustration is *governmental action* (3rd party).
    a. Requirements for Relief
        (1) The use that is frustrated must have been *contemplated by both parties*;
        (2) Frustration must *be total or near total* imposing great hardship;
        (3) The frustrating event must have been *foreseen or foreseeable* by the parties.
    b. Impossibility of Performance
    Also requires a showing of extreme hardship. However, there must be *frustration* of performance, BUT *performance is still possible*.

3. **Destruction of the Premises**
Common law rule is the destruction of the building on the property did not terminate the lease or relieve the T of his obligation to pay rent.
Restatement view is that T may terminate the lease if a change in condition caused by a suddenly non-manmade force makes premises unsuitable for purposes. Impossibility of performance (contract principles). If T causes destruction then T is still under obligation.

4.   Eminent Domain

   a.   Effect of Continuation of Lease
   A permanent taking of all the leased property *extinguishes the leasehold* estate. However, if the government takes the property for a limited period then the lease is *not terminated*.

   b.   Condemnation Award-Rights of Parties
   Lump-sum is given for entire fee simple estate and the award *MUST* be divided between the apportioned interests of the L and the T.

G.   Rights and Duties to Fixture

1.   Fixtures Belong to the Landlord
   Common law is that fixtures cannot be removed for the premises by the T. Fixtures become a part of the realty and the property of L.
   Note: *A "fixture" is usually anything that is permanently attached to the land (i.e. a new wall, new garage).*

2.   Exception - Trade Fixtures
   Those fixtures installed for a particular business purpose are removable as long as no permanent or irreparable damage to the structure.

3.   Modern Trend
   Modern trend is very liberal in allowing T to remove any chattel that he installs as long as the premises can be returned to the their former condition. (Generally, post bond to protect L.)

H.   Duty not to Commit Waste
   Waste defined - action by poss. of land causing injury to other estate holders in property (i.e., L)

1.   Voluntary Waste:
   Willful destruction of premises (active).

2. Permissive Waste:
Allowing leasehold to dillapidate - - waste by omission.

3. Ameliorative Waste:
Defined: Change in physical characteristic of property by unauthorized act of the T, but yet it improves and adds value to leasehold estate. T usually not liable for this because increase in value.

XII   Contract for the Sale of Land

A.   Formalities

1. Statute of Frauds - in NY, GOL 5-703 specifies that the agreement must be in writing and signed by the party to be charged.

2. Binders - Requirements:
    a. Names of ptys.
    b. ID of the land
    c. Promise to buy or sell.
    d. Payment terms - exact.

3. Hiatus between K and closing allows for title search. In every K for the sale of the land, there is implied a promise by the seller that he will deliver on closing good title.

B.   Equitable Conversion

1. As soon as the K is signed, equity regards the K as performed.
    a. Offeree becomes the holder of the realty, and the
    b. Old owner the owner of personalty until closing.

2. Important in 5 contexts:
    a. When a will specifies who will get realty and who will get personalty.
    b. Intestacy taxation.
    c. Dower.
    d. Risk of Loss - between k and closing, at common law risk on seller. NY law says that the party in possession bears risk of loss.
    e. Seller retains legal title as security in an installment land K.

C.   Good Faith

1.   When a buyer in a K makes a promise to buy conditioned upon, for example here, obtaining the proper zoning, there is an implied promise to use good faith and best efforts.
2.   Not doing so is a breach of the K.

D.   When is Title Good Enough, & When Must It Be Marketable?

1.   The idea behind marketable title is that the buyer wants a clear title to the property. *Marketable title* is title free from encumbrances (i.e., liens, mortgages, etc) and any doubts as to its validity. A buyer does not want any "clouds" on the title such as judicial liens, for example because such clouds will mean that the property is worth less or even nothing.

2.   Thus, a *title search* is usually performed as a condition to the sale of land. A title insurance company checks for clouds on the title as a condition to the sale.

3.   In certain instances, when clear title is uncertain, it may be desirable to bring a *bill to quiet title*. A form of a declaratory judgment, the bill resolves who owns the land. Thus, it allows the passing of clear title.

4.   Generally, the owner need only show marketable title upon closing. An exception to the rule that the title need only be marketable at closing is if the seller does something that makes performance unlikely, then the buyer can invoke anticipatory breach.

5.   If the title proves to be encumbered in some manner, the seller and buyer may still choose to carry out the transaction. A buyer's promise to escrow money in the amount of the encumbrance is considered very strong protection. A buyer's promise to indemnify the seller is, however, not that strong in that it is only as good as the promissor

56

E. **Deeds:** **The Instrument of Conveyance**

1. **A deed** is the conveyance of realty that the seller gives to the buyer upon closing.

2. *Merger Doctrine* - in property law, upon closing and accepting the deed all the promises of the contract for sale merge into the deed. Therefore, the only promises that remain are those in the deed itself. To overcome this result, you need merger language to the effect that "these promises shall survive the closing date."

3. *Deed protection* is very weak; it is only as good as the person backing it and the damages are very limited - only the purchase price plus interest.

4. **Types of Deeds:**
   a. *General Warranty Deed* - contains three covenants:
      i. Seisin - possession of the land.
      ii. No Encumbrances
      iii. Warranty by the Owner to pay you the purchase price plus interest if any covenant violated.
   b. *Special Warranty Deed* -
      i. No Encumbrances
      ii. No covenants of seisin or warranty.
   c. *Quitclaim Deed* - I will give you all the interest that I have. A Brooklyn Bridge deed.

5. *Covenants in the Deeds*: (Remember deed damages limited to purchase price & interest.)
   a. *Seisin* -
      i. A present covenant; if breached, breached when made.
      ii. Covenant does not run with the land. Need K to establish.
      iii. Statute of limitations for breach purposes does not begin to run until there has been an eviction.
      iv. What triggers breach is failure of title, either total or partial. Not violated by mortgage or other restriction.

    b. *No Encumbrances -*
       i. A present covenant.
      ii. In NY, the covenant runs with the land, in most other jurisdictions it does not.
     iii. Statute of limitations runs when there is an eviction.
    c. *Warranty Covenant -*
       i. Runs with the land.
      ii. A future covenant, breached when the eviction occurs.
     iii. The damages are awardable to the immediate covenantee or assignee.

F. **Methods of Title Protection**

1. The best method is *title insurance,* which is typically part of a title company's title check. This protection is much stronger than the warranty in a warranty deed.

2. *Recording Statute* – To give notice to all other prospective purchasers of real estate, a deed holder must record his deed. The rationale of recording is to prevent selling the same parcel twice. There are generally two types of recording statutes, and both typically only apply to bona fide, good faith purchasers. These statutes basically prescribe who has a better claim to land. They are:

    a. *Notice statute* – A person with notice of an unrecorded instrument is barred from claiming priority as of the date that on which he received the instrument.
    b. *Race Notice* – first to record the chain of title without notice of a prior unrecorded deed or mortgage has the better rights to the property.
    c. *Race* – whoever records first wins.

3. *Tract System* does not work by grantor-grantee. Rather works by the specific plot involved. Much easier.

4. Generally, an unrecorded deed only binding on grantor, his heirs and devisees.

XIII   Common Methods of Financing Real Estate Purchases: The Mortgage

A. **Purpose of a mortgage** is to finance the purchase of real estate

B. **The Nature of a Mortgage**

1. **Application:** Borrower makes an application to a bank, savings and loan association, etc. The lender uses the information in the application, such as income, assets, liabilities, credit history, and other pertinent financial information to make a determination whether the applicants are an acceptable credit risk.

2. **Evaluation:** If the bank, after evaluation all of the pertinent financial information, feels that the applicants are sound, and approves the loan, the lender will issue a letter of commitment to provide financing for a specified amount on specified terms and within a given period.

3. **Loan:** The bank makes the loan to the purchaser. In return the purchaser/borrower agrees to a twofold obligation. She agrees in a note to pay the lender the amount loaned at a given interest rate over time, usually a 20 or 30 year period. The purchaser/borrower also agrees to give the lender a security interest (a mortgage) in the purchased property for the amount of the loan. (This makes the loan a secured transaction.) Thus *the agreement has two components, the note and the security interest.*

   > Example: Borrower wishes to buy a $250,000 home. Borrower has $50,000 to put down as a down payment. He borrows the remaining $200,000 from a bank at 7% for 30 years. The bank receives a note from the borrower to pay $200,000 at 7% for 30 years, as well as a mortgage (security interest) on the home for $200,000.

4. **The implication** of taking a mortgage is that in the event of default, the lender will be able to collect the amount of the outstanding loan by forcing a sale of the home (the security). The advantage of a mortgage is that in the event of a default on the note the lender will be able to reach the mortgaged property over the other creditors of the borrower.

5. **Terminology:**
    Borrower is referred to as mortgagor.
    Lender is referred to as mortgagee.

C.   Right of Redemption

1. The earliest and classic mortgage was a fee simple deed given to the lender by the borrower, with a condition subsequent clause that if the borrower repaid the lender on the date due, the deed would become void.

2. If the borrower failed to repay the loan, the lender owned the land in fee simple. As the value of the land was almost always more than the amount of the loan, this resulted in a windfall to the lender.

3. Due to the fact that lenders often received a windfall, the chancellor eventually gave the borrower a regular right to redeem the property by paying the lender the amount owed on the loan. This gave the lender his just due, but also avoided unconscionable forfeiture by the borrower.

4. The borrower's ability to redeem the land meant that the lender, while technically holding the property in fee simple, was not secure in his possession of the land. In effect, the lender had title, but the borrower could come along and redeem at any time. To remedy this injustice, the chancellor permitted the borrower's right of redemption to be foreclosed, or ended.

5. The foreclosure of the right of redemption developed into the ordering of a foreclosure sale. A judicial proceeding, the foreclosure proceeding determined the amount of the debt owed the lender and directed an officer of the court to sell the property at a public auction. The proceeds from the sale would go the lender, any remainder to the borrower. (Title to the auctioned property would, of course, go to the auction purchaser.) If the land did not bring enough to satisfy the debt, a deficiency judgment was entered against the borrower.

    a. This practice is now fairly standard in most jurisdictions.

    b. **Note** that an auction sale price that is below what the property would bring in a regular sale is not grounds to set aside the sale, barring fraud or collusion of some type.

6. In about half the states, borrowers were also given a statutory right to redeem the auctioned property from the purchaser who bought it at the auction. Most of these time periods for statutory redemption ranged anywhere from 3 months to 2 years. Note that the statutory right of redemption cannot come into play until there has been a judicial sale.

D. **The Deed of Trust**

1. Because judicial foreclosure involves a lawsuit, and is thus time consuming and expensive, lenders' lawyers sought to circumvent the foreclosure process. Lenders wanted a manner to quickly sell mortgaged land and be paid shortly after a default. They accomplished this goal through a device known as a deed of trust.

2. Under the deed of trust, recognized in a majority of jurisdictions, the borrower conveys title to the land to a person, usually the lender, to hold in trust to secure payment of the debt to the lender. In a deed of trust, the trustee is given the power to sell the land without going to the court if the borrower defaults.

3. Except for the power to foreclose privately which is created by a deed of trust, the deed of trust is treated in all respects as the functional equivalent of a mortgage.

E. Transfers of Mortgaged Property

1. The borrower (mortgagor) may transfer his interest (an equity interest: the value of the property, if any, above the amount of the mortgage) in the land by sale, mortgage, or otherwise. The transfer of the original borrower's interest in the land will not, however, shake off the mortgage. The property remains subject to the mortgage in the hands of the transferee.

2. The purchaser of the equity may buy it either subject to the mortgage, or assuming the mortgage.
   a. *Subject to the mortgage*: purchaser of the equity interest does not assume any personal liability for the mortgage debt, for which the mortgagor remains liable. But the purchaser agrees that the debt will be satisfied out of the land.

   b. *Assuming the mortgage*: purchaser promises to pay off the mortgage debt. This promise gives the mortgagor the right to pay the debt and sue the assuming purchaser for reimbursement. The mortgagee may also enforce the promise made by the purchaser of the equity because she has assumed the obligation to pay.

F. Installment Land Contract

1. Seller contracts to convey title to the purchaser when the purchaser has paid the purchase price in regular installments over a fixed period. When the price is paid in full, the seller agrees to deliver a deed conveying legal title to the purchaser.

2. Little functional difference between installment land contract and ordinary purchase money mortgage. Both devices for securing the payment of unpaid purchase money. Why would one chose an *installment land contract*?
   a. Financing by the seller for those unable to get financing from a bank; or
   b. Buyer may not have sufficient funds for a downpayment.
   c. Favored in jurisdictions where judicial foreclosure is the only method of foreclosing a mortgage.

XIV   Landlord's Remedies

A.   Means of Assuring Performance

1.   Distress (Seizure of T's Chattels)

a. Common Law
If T failed to pay rent, T (without notice) could seize and hold T's chattels as security.

b. Statutory Distress
Most states have *eliminated* the self-help element of the distress doctrine. *Constitution* provides that no state shall deprive any person his property without *due process of law*.

2.   Statutory Liens
Many states create a general lien on T's personal property given the *L priority* over other creditors.

3.   Security Deposits
Lease provisions require that T make deposit when lease is executed and L promises to return money if T has not breached any covenant.

a. Landlord is the Debtor
L owes the money to T at the end of the lease BUT, T as a general creditor, has no priority over any other creditors.

b. Upon Termination of Lease
On termination of the lease the L must return amount that exceeds damages.
Note: *Most states require L to pay interest earned on deposit.*

4. **Rent Acceleration Clauses**
   Standard lease usually provides that the rent for the balance of the term shall become *payable in full upon T's default* in payment of rent or some other obligation.
   Rationale: Since the parties may contract for payment of rent in advance of the lease, they have the right to contract the entire rent payable on a contingency basis.
   Note: *L cannot terminate the lease and accelerate the rent.*

5. **Liquidated Damages**
   L and T may contract in advance on damages for failure to pay rent in limited circumstances. However, the damages MUST be reasonable or ruled as a penalty and not enforceable.

B. **Eviction of Tenant**

   Remember: L's remedies are usually more limited when evicting T *after the term* expires rather than *during the term*.

   1. **Termination for Breach of Covenant**
      Common law allows L's only remedy for failure to pay rent to sue T for the rent.
      The Modern Trend is that most states give L the power to terminate a lease for non-payment when rent is past due.

      a. **Restatement View**
         Dependent covenant doctrine: L may terminate the lease if the promise was a "significant inducement to the making of the lease." (Typically is)

      b. **Lease Provisions**
         Almost every lease contains *express provisions* authorizing L to terminate lease upon the breach of *any covenant*. These provisions for termination (such as "not to keep a dog") are known as *Forfeiture Clauses*.

(1) **Notice of Default and Time to Cure**
Where non-payment is the basis of the forfeiture
→ L must *notify* the T of default, demand rent,
and give a reasonable time to pay.

(2) **Phrased as Determinable Limitation**May
be phrased as a determinable limitation such as "If
T breaches, L *may terminate* after 5 days notice."
Note: L must do something.

(3) **Automatic Termination**
The other way to phrase the lease is that if an
event occurs (X), then the lease automatically
terminates."If T has a dog, the lease terminates
and L re-enters."

c. **Waiver**
L may expressly or impliedly waive her right to
terminate upon breach. *Acceptance of the rent
with knowledge of the breach is considered a
waiver.*
Note: May only waive if a determinable provides for
no waiver because *automatic* this is an advantage to
some L's.

2. **Eviction Through Judicial Process**
Growing minority of states absolutely require L to go to courts
to evict.

a. **Suit in Ejectment**
L may bring an action in ejectment to *recover
possession of the premises*. However, such a trial
takes a while to actually proceed.

b. **Summary Proceedings**
Every state has a summary proceeding allowing L to
recover possession quickly (i.e., action for forcible entry
and detainer).

Some states require use of automatic termination language to summary proceedings as compared to ordinary ejection/eviction.

    (1) **Notice to Quit**
        Most states require that L give notice to T before bringing a summary action but the notice is short because T knows he is acting unlawfully and against the contract.

    (2) **Issues that can be Raised**
        (i)   **Defenses**: T can only use defenses which would preserve his possession and preclude L from regaining.
        (ii)   **Modern Trend**: Some states permit T to defend on grounds that L has breached a duty to repair or habitability.
        (iii)   **Constitutionality**: Any state law that denies T the right to defend on ground that L has breached her duty to repair is constitutional because housing is not a fundamental right.

    (3) **Jury Trial**

3. Self-Help

    a. **Common Law**
    If T had no right to continue possession ‡ common law permitted L to use as much force as reasonably necessary to expel the T.

    b. **Reasonable Force Permitted**
    Some states still follow the reasonable force rule. However, some jurisdictions allow for *peaceable means for entry*.

c. **Self-Help not Permitted**
Modern Trend is to prohibit self-help and require L to turn to the judicial system to seek redresses *first*.
Note: *Self-help allowed if lease contains self-help provision - regardless of lease it would be measured by reasonably necessary force standard.* But, Modern Trend: These are vulnerable to being void on public policy grounds if use force.

d. **Rationale for Eviction over Self-Help**
(1) Violence less likely between L and T.
(2) Summary proceedings are quick, easy and efficient.

C. **Abandonment by Tenant**
If T has no right to vacate the property but abandon it, L has several options:

1. **Landlord Terminates Lease (Surrender)**
L may terminate the lease upon T's abandonment; this effects a *surrender*. T is only liable for rents accrued and for damages caused by abandonment - no future rents liable.

a. **Common Law Rule**
L cannot terminate the lease and can receive damages for anticipatory breach of contract for remainder of lease term.

b. **Anticipatory Repudiation Allowed**
In some states anticipatory repudiation is allowed by L when T make it clear that he will pay no further rent (i.e. abandonment).

2. **Landlord Stands By and Does Nothing**
L may leave the premises vacant and sue the T for rent as it comes due under the lease. This is the common law viewpoint.
Note: *Modern trend is that L has a duty to mitigate damages. Very much like contract principles.* Modern trend generally towards K law.

3. Landlord Repossesses and Re-leases
L may enter and repossess the property for the purpose of renting it out to another T. Courts are divided as to whether this effects a *surrender and thus terminates the lease*.

    a. **Re-leasing Effects Surrender**
Some courts view re-leasing as a surrender unless T expressly or impliedly consents to the re-lease.

    b. **Re-leasing Without Notice Effects Surrender**
If L gives notice of the re-leasing and notice that she intends to hold T for any loss in rents, L may re-lease for T's benefit but still collect on any deficiencies. The L is hold to "good faith" standard. If L re-leases at a lower cost purposely then L loses any right to collect deficient rent from T.

XV. Assignment and Subletting

> SUBLEASE → T transfers less than the leasehold. T has a reversion.
> ASSIGNMENT → T transfers entire term – no interest is retained.
>
> MODERN RULE: Court will look to:
> (1) Intention of the parties;
> (2) Surrounding circumstances.

A. Assignment

If T assigns his leasehold, the assignee comes into **privity of estate** with L, which means that the landlord and the assignee are liable to each other on the covenants in the original lease that run with the land.

1. Privity of Estate
An ancient concept developed to give the L the right to sue the assignee of the T on the covenants in the lease, and to give assignee the right to sue the L on his covenants.

2. Privity of Contract
If there is privity of contract, their obligations bind them regardless of whether or not they are in privity of estate.

> **ASSIGNMENT**
> (1) Privity of Estate between L and T1 ends; Privity of Estate between L and T2 which means that they are liable to each other; Privity of Contract between L and T1 survives
> (2) T2 not in Privity of Contract with L unless he expressly assumes duties of original lease.
> (3) L may only proceed in action against T in which there was Privity of Estate OR Privity of Contract.
> For example, L leases to T. T assigns the leasehold to T2. L and T1 have Priority of Contract – L and T2 have Privity of Estate.
> **SUBLEASE**
> (1) L and T1 remain both in Privity of Estate and Contract.
> (2) L would have to proceed against T1 in any action. T2 would be a third party to the original lease.

B. **Sublease Distinguished from Assignment**
T becomes **landlord of the subleasee.** The subleasee is not in privity of estate with the L and cannot sue or be sued by the L.

1. **Reversion Retained**
At common law, a transfer by a T is a sublease **if T retains a reversion** in the property after the transfer. A reversion is a period of time within the duration of the leasehold when T will again be entitled to possession.

2. **Right of Entry Retained**

  a. **Common Law View**
  If right of reentry was retained (usually based on condition of rent being paid) → the court would find it to be an assignment because no reversion is retained.

  b. **Right of Entry Makes it a Sublease**
  Modern Courts hold the reservation of right to reenter for nonpayment of rent is deemed a **contingent reversionary interest** and is thus considered a **sublease**.

3. **Intention Controls**
Modern cases also articulate that reversionary interest is not necessary because it is judged by *INTENT* of the parties.

C. **Duty to Pay Rent**
A promise to pay rent is covenant running with the land, which means the promisee can sue any person on the covenant with whom she is in privity of estate.
General Rule: L can sue for rent any person who is either in **privity of contract** with the L as to rent obligations, **OR** who has come into **privity of estate** with L so as to be bound by rental covenants in the lease.

1. **Assignment**
Establishes **privity of estate** between the L and the assignee, so that assignee is personally responsible for the rent even though no mention is made of it in the assignment.

a. **Liability of Original T**
   Original T also remains liable for the rent, in the event the assignee fails to pay, because the **original T contracted with the L.**
   (1) T is surety
   (2) Release by L (effect)
       Only way T can escape from his duty to pay rent is by an express or implied **release** from his promise to L. Consent to assignment doesn't allow for implied release.
   (3) Novation
       Novation if T1 is released and T2 becomes solely responsible for the lease.

b. **Liability of Assignee**
   T2 is only liable for rent accruing during the time he hold the leasehold. Not responsible for rent accruing prior to assignment time.

2. **Sublease**
   If T subleases, the sublessee is not personally liable to the L for rent.

   a. **Rationale**
      There is neither privity of contract or estate between T2 and L.

   b. **Lien on Rental**
      Although the L cannot sue the sublessee for rent, L may have equitable remedies that protect her if she doesn't want to terminate the master lease. L can assert an equitable lien on rent due under sublease, so she has priority over the T-Sublessor's creditors.

D. **Covenants Against Assignment or Sublease**
Absent any covenant to the contrary, a leasehold is **freely transferable** by the T.

1. **Express Covenants**
Such covenants are allowed but **strictly construed because of their restraint on alienation**.

2. **Arbitrary Denial of Consent**
If there is a covenant against transfer without L's consent, the older view is that the L **may arbitrarily refuse to accept** a new T.
Newer view is generally, L simply agrees, but T must give notice. Typically in real property leases.

3. **Waiver of Covenant**
L may expressly or, by her acts, impliedly waive the covenant against assignment or sublease. Implied waiver usually occurs when the landlord **accepts rent from the assignees with knowledge of the assignment**.

E. **Covenants Running to Assignees (Privity of Estate)**

1. **Introduction**
For L to be able to enforce a covenant in the lease against T's assignee, or for the T to be able to enforce a covenant in the lease against the L's assignee, the following requirements must be met:

a. **Intention**
The parties to the lease must intend that the covenant runs to assignees.

b. **Privity of Estate**
Assignee must be in either privity of estate or privity of contract with the person who is suing or being sued. Privity of estate means, that the person succeeded to the estate of a party to the contract. If the assignee has

74

promised to perform the covenant, the assignee's liability rests on privity of contract.

Example:

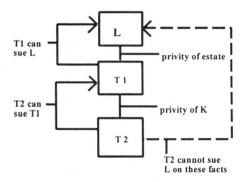

T1 can sue L

privity of estate

T2 can sue T1

privity of K

T2 cannot sue L on these facts

c. Touch and Concern
Covenant must directly affect the party in the **use or enjoyment of the property**.

(1) Two ends to covenant - Burden and Breach
Whoever makes the promise has the **burden**.
Whoever has promise make has the **benefit**.

(2) Generally both burden and benefit touch and concern lease land.
In majority of covenants, if either end touches and concerns, the other will also, because the covenant will have some direct relationship to the use or enjoyment of the premises.

(3) Personal covenant
If a covenant does not touch and concern the promisor's interest, it is personal to the promisor. The promisor continues to be liable on the personal promise after assignment if the parties intended.

d. Notice
To be liable, the assignee must have notice of the promise sued upon. Notice may be implied under circumstances where the assignee should have made reasonable inquiry and, if he had, would have discovered the promise (*Constructive Notice*).

2. Covenant to do or not to do a Physical Act on the Lease Premises
Such acts include covenants to repair, to conduct business in certain manner, not to remove fixtures, to furnish heat and to deliver up premises in good condition.

a. Runs with Leasehold
A covenant **by the T or by the L** to do or refrain from doing a physical act **on the leased premises** touches and concerns the land and runs with it.

b. Runs with Reversion
If L or T makes a covenant to do or not to do a physical act **on the leased land**, the covenants runs to assigns of the reversion.

3. Covenants to Pay Money
Connected to rent or land in other way. Run with the land.

4. Tenant's Covenant to Insure for Benefit for Landlord

Insurance Proceeds used for Rebuilding
A covenant by T to insure the property touches and concerns **if** the lease requires the L to use the proceeds for rebuilding.

5. Landlord's Covenant to Return a Security Deposit
A covenant by L to repay a security deposit at the end of the lease has been held by some courts to be a personal promise that does not run with the land.

XVI.   Easements

A. Introduction

1. Definition
An easement is a grant of an interest in land that entitles a person to use land possessed by another.

2. Types of Easements

a. Affirmative Easement
Owner of an affirmative easement has the right to **go onto the land** of another and do some act on the land (most easements are affirmative).

b. Negative Easements
The owner of a negative easement can **prevent the owner** or the servient land from doing some act on the servient land. Negative easements are rare and usually not permitted unless one of the five types listed below:
- Light
- Air Flow
- Subjacent or Lateral Support
- Flow of Artificial Stream
- Scenic View

(1) Why types are limited
Almost all types of purported negative easements can be treated as **promises** by the servient owner not to use his land in a certain way. If A promises not to do something he would be creating a covenant not an easement.

(2) Compare - affirmative act by servient owner
If the owner or the servient land agrees to perform an affirmative act on the servient land, this is a covenant, not an easement. An easement involves either the right of A to on O's servient land or the right of A to prohibit O's use of his land in a way resembling one of the five ways of negative easements.

3. **Easements Appurtenant or In-Gross**

    a. **Easement Appurtenant**
If an easement benefits its owner **in the use of another tract of land**, it is appurtenant to that land (convenant in land). The land benefited is called **the dominant tenement**; the land burdened is the **servient tenement**.

        (1) Passes with dominant tenement
Easements appurtenant is attached to the dominant tenement and passes with the tenement to any subsequent owner of the tenement. It cannot be separated from the dominant tenement and turned into an easement in-gross, unless the owners of the dominant and servient tenements make a new agreement permitting it.

        (2) Negative Easement
A negative easement is *always appurtenant* to land. It protects the owner of the easement in his enjoyment of land.

    b. **Easement in Gross**
Does not belong to person by virtue of ownership of another estate; rather a personal right in property. *See, e.g. Shingleton v. State*, 130 SE 2d 183, 185-86.
Does not benefit its owner in the use and enjoyment of land, but merely *gives him the right to use the servient land*. For example, public utilities.

    c. **Easement Appurtenant Favored**
If instrument is ambiguous then courts generally construe it as creating an easement appurtenant.

        (1) Rationale
            (i) Intention
Parties usually have a dominant tenement in mind. If the easement serves to benefit the use of a tract of land or serves to enhance the value of a neighboring tract then it is appurtenant.

      (ii) History
          English courts refuse to recognize easements in gross.

      (iii) Elimination of obsolete easements
          It is thought to be easier to eliminate an obsolete easement appurtenant because it can follow the land title chain, and the benefited party, who can release it, will be more easily ascertainable than the owners of the easement in gross.

      (iv) Land Value Increase
          Easement appurtenant increases the value of the dominant land.

4. Interest in Land

An easement is an interest in land. This means that *the burden passes to the owners of the servient land*. The owner of and easement does not merely have contract rights against original grantor of the easement, but also has rights against all successors to the grantor.

5. Profit Compared

A profit is the *right to take something off* another person's land that is part of the land or a product of the land (i.e., timber, minerals, wild game, fish).

In Gross Preferred

Although a profit can be appurtenant to other land, the usual profit is in gross. A profit is usually not intended to benefit the owner of it in the use of adjacent land but rather intended to give the owner an economically valuable item.

6. License Compared

A license is ***permission*** to upon land belonging to the licensor. Can be oral or written. A license is ***revocable*** at the will of the licensor. *See, e.g., Logan v. McGee*, 320 So. 2d 792, 793-94. for comparison of license to easement.

a. Construction

Cases arise where the issue is whether a person has a license or an easement in gross. If it is a license, it is not binding on the new owner of the land, BUT if it is an easement, it is binding on a new owner who has notice of it. ***NOTE: Courts usually determine it as a license.***

b. Irrevocable License

(1) License coupled with an interest

A license coupled with an interest cannot be revoked because it gives the right to remove a chattel of the licensee, which is on the licensor's property. For example, O sells A a care on O's land → A has irrevocable license to enter and remove the car.

(2) Estoppel

A license may become irrevocable under the rules of estoppel. If the licensee has constructed substantial improvements on either the licensor's land or the licensee's land, relying on the license, a licensor may be estopped from revoking the license.

c. Theater Tickets

Courts have held that a ticket creates an irrevocable license, but this is not an interest in land so as to permit self help in removing someone from your seat.

d. Assignability

A license is presumed to be personal and nonassignable, but if the parties so intend, it can be made transferable.

B. Creation of Easements

1. Creation by Express Grant

a. Statute of Frauds
An easement, being an interest in land, must satisfy the Statute of Frauds. Creation of an easement requires a *written interest signed by the grantor.* **NOTE:** *If the grantor doesn't sign a written instrument but orally gives the grantee permission to enter the land → grantee has a license.*

b. Duration of Easement
An easement can be treated as to last any amount of time.

c. Construction of Ambiguous Instrument
Difficult to tell whether the grantor intended to create an easement or a fee simple. Generally, a grant of *limited use*, or for a *limited purpose*, or of an identified space *without clearly marked boundaries* creates an easement.

2. Creation by Reservation
An easement may be reserved by the grantor over the land granted in fee simple. If the grantor conveys land, reserving an easement, the land conveyed is the servient tenement.
Reservation in Favor of Third (3rd) Party
Common Law: an easement could not be reserved in favor of a third party.
Modern: Still a majority rule.

a. Solution: Draft Around it Using Two (2) Instruments
First document transfers interest in property from grantor to grantee.
Second document transfers easement from grantee to third party.

b. Compare with Covenant
Covenant can be created in the interest of a third party.

c. Minority
Allow third party benefits. *Rationale is without allowing interest in third party, the third party would pay for the value of the easement without receiving it.*

3. Creation by Implication
An easement by implication is created by *operation of law*, not by a written instrument. It is an exception to the Statute of Frauds. However, an easement can be implied only in very narrowly defined circumstances indicating that the parties intended an easement or that an easement is a necessity (Quasi-easement).

a. Easement Implied from Existing Use
If, prior to the time a tract of land is divided into two lots, a use exists on the "servient part" that is reasonably necessary for the enjoyment of the "dominant part" and which the court finds the parties intended to continue after the tract is divided, an easement may be implied. *See, e.g., Schwab v. Green*, 215 NW2d 240, 241-42.

(1) Implied only over Land Granted or Reserved when Tract is Divided
An easement can only be implied over land granted or reserved when a tract is divided into two or more lots.
Implied in favor of grantee is an implied grant.
Implied in favor of grantor is an implied reservation.

(2) Existing Use at Time of Tract Division
When a tract is divided a use of one part of the tract must exist from which it can be inferred that an easement permitted its continuation was intended. This existing use is often called *a quasi-easement*.

(i) Apparent
To have a quasi-easement, the previous use must be apparent. It is apparent if the grantee could, by reasonable inspection of

the premises, discover the existence of the use.

(ii) Continuous
The previous use must be *continuous*, not sporadic. It insures that the parties knew the existence of use at the time of the grant.

(3) Reasonable Necessity
The easement must be necessary for the enjoyment of the claimed dominant tenement. Necessity is important because it effects the intent of the parties. *Only reasonable necessity*, not strict necessity.

b. **Easement by Necessity**
An easement by necessity is implied if the owner of a tract of land divides the tract into two lots and deprives one lot of access to a public road. Must be strictly necessary *and not just a more convenient access*. Courts base implied easement on *public policy* and *intent of the parties*. *Stated differently - easement that is essential to the enjoyment of the dominant estate.*

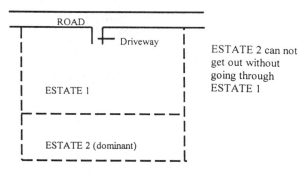

(1) Implied only over Landlocked Parcels
The necessity must *exist when the land is divided*. The easement is only implied over that portion that blocks access to a public road from the

landlocked parcel. *Only lasts as long as there is a necessity.* If another public road is built so that the landlocked parcel has access, the easement dies.

    (2)   No Existing Use Required
An easement by necessity, unlike an easement implied on the basis of existing use, does not require an existing use at time land is divided.

    (3)   Location of Easement
The owner of the servient parcel has the right to locate the easement by necessity, provided the location is reasonably convenient. Best capable of locating easement so as to do the least amount of damage or disturbance to servient parcel.

    (4)   Easement other than Ways
An easement by necessity might be implied in situations where an easement for something other than road access is claimed such as for a sewer. Modern courts usually don't allow such an easement because sewage can be removed by trucks.

    (5)   Termination by Necessity
Last only so long as it is necessary.

4. Creation by Prescription
Long use leads to easement (implied).

a. Historical Development
The same policies that underlie the law of adverse possession apply to long use of an easement. Thus, the courts developed the doctrine that an easement could be acquired by prescription by an *adverse user* for a requisite period of time.

    (1)   English Law
Fiction of the Lost Grant: If a person has been using another's land for the requisite period of time, the court will presume that she was doing so under a grant from some former owner, which grant is now lost.

(2)   American Law
Resembles the law of adverse possession. If the statute of limitations for adverse possession is 20 years, then the prescriptive period for acquiring an easement is 20 years.

b.   Elements of Prescription

(1)   ***Open and Notorious Use***
Use must be made without any attempt at concealment. (Often litigated in cases involving underground sewers and drains).

(2)   ***Under a Claim of Right***
Must be under a claim of right and ***not with permission of the owner***. Same as adverse possession → court may apply an ***objective or subjective test.***
OBJECTIVE: appears to be under a claim of right to community.
SUBJECTIVE: user must have good faith belief that he has a right to use the land.

  (i)   Permissive Use Changes Adverse
If a person uses the land with the permission of another and later begins to do acts that should reasonably put the owner on notice that the user is ***claiming a right*** to the use of land → the use becomes adverse.

  (ii)   Color of Title
Some states require color of title and payment of taxes for adverse possession. ***Neither is required*** for prescriptive easement.

(3)   ***Continuous Use***
Must be continuous use but not constant because of an easement ordinarily involves only periodic use. Continuity requires a ***continuous claim***

85

> *of right and periodic acts which give notice to the owner.*
> (i) Seasonal use meets the requirement.
> (ii) Occasional and sporadic trespass is not enough.
> (iii) Tacking is allowed in prescription just as it is in adverse possession.

(4) *Uninterrupted Use*
Once the adverse use is interrupted by the owner of the land being used, the prescriptive period ends. If adverse use begins again after interruption, a new prescriptive period begins.

c. **When Prescriptive Rights cannot be Acquired**
(1) Negative Easements
Negative easements (for light, air, drainage or support) *cannot* arise by prescription. The reason is that prescription *bars a cause of action* and where the owner has no cause of action, prescription does not apply.
(2) Easement by Necessity
Use of an easement by necessity *cannot* give rise to a prescriptive easement. This is because the use of an easement by *necessity is by right and not wrongful.* However, when the necessity ends, the easement by necessity also ends.
(3) Public Lands
Cannot obtain prescriptive rights here.

d. **Public Easements**
In most jurisdictions, the *public at large can acquire a public easement* in private land by prescription if members of the public use the private land in a manner meeting the requirements for prescription.
(1) Minority View
General public cannot acquire prescriptive rights in private property. Rationale being that owner's

cause of action runs against the specific trespassing of individuals and not against the public at large.

(2) Customary Rights

If the public has used the beach (dry sand in private ownership) for so long that "the memory of may runneth not the contrary," the public has a *customary right to the use of the beach.* *Matthews v. Bay Head Improvement Association,* 95 N.J. 306, 471 A.2d 355.

C. Scope of Easements

1. General Rule

Scope of an easement *depends upon the intention of the parties.* In interpreting the intentions, the court looks to:

a. How the easement depends was created (expressly or by prescription);
b. What changes in use are reasonably foreseeable by the parties;
c. What changes in use are required to achieve the purposes of the easement;
d. Whether the increase in use reasonable.

2. How easement was created

a. Express Easement

If the easement was *expressly* created, the court will look at the *language of the instrument*, together with the *surrounding circumstances* to decide the parties' intent.

Easement of Use

An easement of way is a favorite of the law because surface access is essential to the *use and productivity of land*. It is given a scope that permits it to meet the needs of the dominant tenement as it normally develops.

b. **Implied Easements**
  (1) Existing Use
      If an easement is implied *on the basis of a use existing at the time of severance of a tract into two parcels that the parties intended to continue*, the scope is generally the same as an express easement. Changes that are reasonably expected or that are necessary to preserve the utility of the easement are permitted.
  (2) Easement by Necessity
      The *extent of the necessity* determines the scope.

3. **Easements by Prescription**
   It is *more difficult* to increase the burden of an easement by prescription than any other type of easement. The use that gives rise to the easement can continue, but there is no basis for assuming the parties intended the easement to accommodate future needs. For example, if a prescriptive easement is acquired by use to reach a house and the use of the dominant tenement is changed from residential to commercial → added burden of traffic will not be permitted.

4. **Subdivision by the Dominant Tenement**
   General Rule: If the dominant tenement estate is subdivided then each subdivided lot has a right to use easements appurtenant to the dominant estate. *An easement is appurtenant to every part of the dominant estate.*
   Exception: The servient estate is *NOT* to be burdened to a greater extent than was contemplated at the time of the easement was created.

5. **Use for Benefit of Non-dominant Land**
   An easement granted for the benefit of lot 1 cannot be used for the benefit of lot 2, even though the same person owns lots 1 and 2. *The dominant owner cannot increase the scope of the easement by using it to benefit a non-dominant tenement.*

6. Change in Location of Easement

If an easement has been granted in a specific location, or has been located by mutual agreement of the parties, the location *cannot* thereafter be changed by one party acting unilaterally. The location can be changed only by *mutual consent*.

7. Widening of Easement

Easements cannot be widened without consent of *servient owner*.

8. Use by Servient Owner

The servient owner has the right to use the servient land in ways that do not *unreasonably* interfere with the easement (i.e. servient may erect a structure over easement of way as long as enough room for passage of vehicles.

9. Easements and Profits in Gross

Easements and profits in gross present a special problem about excessive use, since the use is not limited by the needs of a dominant tenement.

  a. Nonexclusive Use

  If an easement or profit in gross is *nonexclusive* (i.e. enjoyed by beneficiary and the servient owner) *it cannot be apportioned*. Absent authority in the grant, the owner of the easement or profit cannot convey to two or more persons the right to share in its use.

  b. Exclusive Use

  If beneficiary has an exclusive right to enjoy the easement or profit, it can be apportioned or divided by the owner. The owner can grant the right to others to share its use as long as the original grant does not prohibit it.

10. One Stock Rule

When two or more persons own an easement or profit in gross, they must use the easement or profit as one stock. Neither can operate independently of the other. The consent of ALL is required.

D. Transfer of Easements

1. Easement Appurtenant

When the dominant tenement is transferred then any easements appurtenant are transferred with it. Similarly, the **burden** of an easement appurtenant passes with the servient land when transferred. *RULE: Easement appurtenant is "attached" to the dominant land.*

Detachment - Easements can be detached with the consent of both parties.

2. Easements in Gross

Courts have restricted the transfer of easements in gross because of the difficulty of locating the large number of people it may be assigned.

Commercial Easements in Gross Assignable

Modern Rule: Commercial easement in gross is assignable and a non-commercial easement is assignable if the parties so intend. Commercial easement are those which have a primary economic benefit rather than personal satisfaction.

Rationale: It would be inefficient public policy for a transportation or utility company to lose its easement when it merged with another company.

3. Profits in Gross

Profits in gross have always been assignable.

E Termination of Easements

1. By Unity of Title

An easement is a right in land of *another*. If title to the easement and the servient tenement come into the same hands then the easement is extinguished. (Usually occurs when the same person buys the dominant and servient tenements). The easement *is not revived* by further division or re-division of the property. However, can of course, establish a different easement.

2 . By Acts of Dominant Owner

a . Release
The owner of an easement may release the easement to the servient owner by a *written instrument*. (Oral release is ineffective due to the Statute of Frauds). However, the easement may be estopped if released orally and the servient tenement spends money or relies detrimentally on the oral assertion.

b . Non-Use
Mere non-use of the easement *does not* extinguish the easement.

c . Abandonment
Oral release or non-use is not sufficient alone *BUT* if the owner acts in such a way as to indicate an *unequivocal intent* to abandon the easement then the easement is abandoned. Rationale: Abandonment of easement removes an encumbrance on the title and makes the land more marketable.

d . Alteration of Dominant Tenement
If an easement is granted for a particular purpose, and an alteration of the dominant tenement makes it impossible to achieve the purpose any longer then the easement is extinguished. Courts are reluctant to construe an easement for one particular purpose.

e . Easement by Necessity
Terminates when the necessity ends. For example, if a dominant owner acquires new ways of access through conveyances or prescription.

3 . By Acts of the Servient Owner

a . Destruction of Servient Tenement
An easement in a structure is terminated if the building is destroyed without the fault of the owner of the servient

estate. If the building is destroyed by an ***intentional act***, then the easement is not extinguished.

b. Prescription
If the servient owner interferes with an easement in an adverse manner, the servient owner can extinguish the easement by prescription (i.e., by erecting a fence across the roadway).

4. Eminent Domain
Eminent domain terminates an easement.

5. Express Condition
If there is an express condition in the granting instrument and that condition is violated or satisfied then the easement terminates.

XVII.   Real Covenants

A. Introduction

1. What are Covenants?
A covenant is a promise to do or not to do a certain thing.
Affirmative promise → *promise to do something.*
Negative promise → *promise not to do something.*
If the promisee sues the promisor for breach, the law of contracts is applicable. If, however, a person who buys the *promisee's land* is suing or a person who buys the *promisor's land* is being sued ‡ the law of property is applicable.

2. Remedies for Breach: Only get money damages.
Money damages must be sued for *in law*.

3. Real Covenant Defined
A real covenant is a covenant that runs with the land *at law*, so that, each person who owns the land subsequently is entitled to enforce or is burdened by the covenant. A real covenant is one that is enforceable at law by a successor owner of the promisee's property and concomitantly, is enforceable against a successor to the promisor's land.

4. Distinguished from Other Interests

a. Equitable Servitude
An equitable servitude is a covenant enforceable *in equity* by or against successors to land of the original parties to the contract.

b. Easement
A covenant is a *promise* respecting the use of land, and an easement is a *grant of interest* in land. An affirmative easement gives someone the right to go on another's land, which a covenant never does. On the other hand, a negative easement resembles a promise not to do something.

93

c. **Condition**
A condition provides for *forfeiture* upon breach of the condition, whereas a covenant is enforceable by an award or money damages.

5. **Benefit and Burden Explained**
In the law of easements, one parcel is the *servient or burdened tenement* and the other is the *dominant or benefited tenement*. Under covenants, the talk only concerns the benefit or the burden.

B. **Creation**

1. **Writing Required (The Deed)**
At common law a real covenant had to be in writing and under seal.
Note: Covenants *can not* be implied or arise by prescription.

2. **Grantee Bound without Signing**
Most deeds are only signed by the grantor. Such a deed is known as a deed poll. By accepting the deed poll, the grantee is bound by any covenants in the deed to be performed by the grantor.

C. **Enforcement By or Against Assignees**
Major Issue: Whether the covenant can be enforced by a successor to the promisee or against a successor to the promisor?
REMEMBER: Requirements for the burden to run to assignees are more exacting than for the benefit to run.

1. **Requirements for the Burden to Run at Law**

a. **Intent**
The contracting parties must intend that successors to the promisor will be bound by the covenant. This is usually

indicated by the language binding the ***promisor and their "heirs or assigns."***

b. **Privity of Estate**
Majority of courts require privity of estate between the *original promisor and the promisee*, as well as privity of estate between the *promisor and his assignees.*
(1) **Horizontal** (promisor and promisee): and
(2) **Vertical** (Origional party and assignee).

c. **Touch and Concern the Land**
The covenant must touch and concern the burdened land. In a majority of states, the covenant must touch and concern the benefited land as well. NOTE: The burden will not run if the benefit is in gross.
TEST: ***Whether a covenant substantially alters the legal rights of the owner?***

d. **Notice**
A subsequent purchaser of the promisor's land is not bound by the burden unless he has notice of the covenant before buying.

2. **Requirements for Benefit to Run at Law**

a. **Intent**
The contracting parties must intend that the benefit run to successor of the promisee.

b. **Privity of Estate (vertical only)**
Privity estate between the original contracting parties is NOT required for the benefit to run. *However, privity between the promisee and the assignee is required.*

c. **Touch and Concern**
Benefit must touch and concern the land owned by the promisee.

3. Intention of Parties
Usually found in the language of a deed or contract. If the instrument is unclear the court will look at:
   a. *The purpose of the covenant; and*
   b. *All the related circumstances.*

4. Privity of Estate
Horizontal → privity between promisor and promisee
Vertical → privity between an original party and assignee.

Requirements to Run	
Burden	Benefit
(1) Intent	(1) Intent
(2) Notice	(2) Touch and Concern
(3) Touch and Concern	(3) Vertical Privity
(4) Horizontal Privity	
(5) Vertical Privity	

   a. Horizontal Privity - Relationship Between the Contracting Parties
   (1) Running of the Burden
       For the **burden** of a covenant to run to assignees, the majority rule is that the original parties to the covenant must be in privity of estate.
       (i) English View
           The parties to a promise are in privity of estate only if they are in a landlord and tenant relationship.
       (ii) Mutual Interest
           A few states took the position that what put the parties in privity of estate was the fact that the landlord and tenant both have an interest in the property. Applying this view, the burden will run if one party has an interest in the land of the other.
       (iii) Successive Relationship
           Majority Rule: Important that the covenant was contained in a **conveyance**

of an interest in land. Applying this view to a covenant by a fee owner, privity of estate is present where the promise is contained in a conveyance of the fee simple (i.e. where one of the original parties to the promise succeeds to an estate previously owned by the other parties).

(iv) Restatement View
Privity of estate is satisfied by either a mutual relationship or a successive relationship.

(v) Minority View
Minority view holds that horizontal privity is not necessary.

b. Vertical Privity - the Interest Transferred to the Assignee
For an assignee **to sue** on a covenant at law, the **assignee** must be in privity of estate with the original **promisee**. Also, for an assignee to be sued on a covenant, the assignee must be in privity of estate with the original promisor.

(1) Running of the Burden
When the assignment of the burden is the issue → Restatement defines vertical privity to mean **succession to the estate** of one of the original parties. Restatement § 535.
REMEMBER: The assignee must succeed to the **identical estate** owned by the promisor.

(2) Running of the Benefit
Restatement says the benefit will run to assigns of the original estate or of **any lesser estate**, such as a life estate. The owner of any succeeding possessory estate can enforce the benefit at law.

5. Touch and Concern
For the burden to run with the burdened land, the covenant must touch and concern the burdened land. This requirement is usually discussed with **equitable servitudes**.

6. Notice
A bona fide purchaser of the burdened land **is not bound at law** if he has no notice of the covenant.

7. Liability of Original Promisor After Assignment
The answer depends on the type of promise made:

    a. Promise to Perform Act
    If the covenant is a promise to do or not to do some act on the burdened land, then the covenantor has **no liability** after the assignment. The covenantor has no control over the land after assignment, so it would be unfair to hold him liable for performance of the covenant by the assignee or subsequent assignment.

    b. Promise to Pay Money
    If the covenant is a promise to pay money, the covenantor **may be liable** after assignment on the theory that his personal credit may have been important to the deal, or that his lack of control over the land does not prevent performance.

XVIII.   Equitable Servitudes

A. Introduction

1. Definition

An equitable servitude is a covenant, whether running with the land at law or not, that equity will enforce against **assignees** of the burdened land who have **notice** of the covenant. The usual equitable remedy granted is an **injunction** against violation of the covenant.

2. Historical Development

Because England had no recording system through which subsequent purchasers could learn about covenants applicable to the land, they would not allow a covenant by a fee simple owner to run with land to an assignee.

a. Tulk v. Moxhay, 2 Phil.Ch 774, 41 Eng. Rep. 1143 (1848)

Tulk sold a square to Elms, who promised for himself, his heirs and assigns, not to build on the square. Moxhay was a subsequent purchaser who had notice of the covenant but proposed to build on the land anyway. Tulk sought an injunction to stop the building. The court felt it would be inequitable to not to enforce the covenant against Moxhay because:

    a.   He had notice; and

    b.   He probably paid less for the land because of the covenant.

b. Theory of Enforcement

The right to specific performance of the contract was deemed to give the promisee an interest in the land. When the promise was negative, the right was thought of as an "equitable interest analogous to a negative easement."

3. Equitable Servitude Compared with Real Covenants

If a promisee **seeks damages** from an assignee, the promisee must go into law and attempt to enforce the promise as a real covenant. If the promisee seeks an **injunction** the promisee must go into equity and ask for enforcement of an equitable servitude.

a. **Remedies Compared**
    In the usual case, the plaintiff wants an injunction, not damages. An injunction is worth more to the plaintiff than damages.

b. **Creation**
    A real covenant must be in writing. In many states, an equitable servitude must also be in writing because it is an interest in land and subject to the Statute of Frauds.

c. **Privity of Estate**
    Neither horizontal nor vertical privity of estate is required in equity. The court is enforcing an interest in land analogous to an easement, which is enforceable against any person who interferes with it.

d. **Identical Requirements**
    Both real covenants and equitable servitudes require that the covenant touch and concern the land. Neither is enforceable against a bona fide purchaser without notice.

B. **Creation**
    Most courts hold that the Statute of Frauds requires a writing signed by the promisor. As with real covenants, acceptance of the deed only signed by the grantor binds the grantee as the promisor. Exception: *Negative equitable servitudes* may be implied from a common scheme for development of a residential subdivision.

    1. **Negative Servitude Implied from a Scheme**
        In the case of a restricted residential subdivision, many courts will imply a negative servitude on a lot even though there is no writing creating the servitude on that lot. Usually done on a theory of *equitable estoppel*: purchaser buying a lot in that

area relies on the promise of the subdivider to restrict the other lots to residential use.

a. **The Circumstances**
   Suppose a developer subdivides 50 lots and sells 30 with oral promise that all the lots will be for residential use. The developer sells 2 corner lots to gas companies. If (1) the developer had a *scheme* of residential subdivision and (2) the gas companies had *notice* of the covenants of the other 30 lots, then the courts will imply a covenant on the gas companies.

   Two Requirements:
   (1) Must be a scheme; and
   (2) Must be sufficient evidence of the scheme (i.e., pretty obvious if 30 lots surrounding the land is residential).

b. **Kind of Servitude Implied**
   A servitude similar to a *reciprocal negative easement* is implied. The servitude must be *reciprocal* (i.e., covenant binds all lots in a subdivision). It must be a *negative or restrictive covenant* → the court will not imply an affirmative covenant.

   Evidence of a Scheme:
   (1) Plat with restrictions;
   (2) Exhibition of a developer's map;
   (3) Oral representation of others;
   (4) Ads and brochures; and
   (5) Many other lots who are uniform in quality.

2. **Real Covenants**
   Real covenants will not be implied in any state because the courts deem it unfair to impose unlimited personal liability upon a person without an express agreement. An injunction limits liability to the value of the land.

C. **Enforcement By or Against Assignee**
To enforce you need:

1. **A Writing**

2. **Intent**
The contracting parties must intend that the servitude be enforceable by and against assignees. No technical words are needed.

3. **Privity of Estate**

    a. **Between Covenantor and Covenantee**
Horizontal privity is NOT required for the burden of a covenant to run to assigns is equity. Equity is enforcing a property interest analogous to an easement, and no special relationship between the parties who created the property interest is necessary.

    b. **Between Covenanting Party and Assignee**
Equity does not require vertical privity of estate between a covenanting party and an assignee. In law, the court views the covenant as attaching to and running with an estate in land. Equity is enforcing a servitude in the nature of an easement in the servient estate.

4. **Touch and Concern Requirement**

    a. **General Rule**
For the burden to run in equity and in law → the covenant must touch and concern the land.
Old Rule: Whether the covenant burdens or benefits a party in the *physical use or enjoyment* of a particular land.
Modern: Whether the covenant *enhances the value* of the particular land.

        Function Requirement
Function is to permit courts to stop covenants from running when the social utility of the

covenant is outweighed by the fettering of the burdened property. Most courts look to the decision that would be reached by the present landowners in a negotiation of the transaction costs. For example, if the value of the benefited exceeds the burden, the present landowners would reimpose the covenant because it would be to the advantage of both.

b . Specific Applications
    (1)   Negative Covenants
        Covenants not to do a physical act does touch and concern the land. Restrictive covenants *enhance the value* of the benefited land.
            (i)   Covenants Not to Compete - Burden Side
                A covenant not to compete restricts the promisor in the *physical use* he may make of his land. Hence, it touches and concerns the *burdened estate* as much as a covenant restricting the property to residential use.
            (ii) Covenants Not to Compete - Benefit Side
                Covenant not to compete enhances the value of the covenantee's land, but it is debatable whether it affects the physical use of his property. Nevertheless, a majority of courts hold that *enhancement of commercial value* satisfies the requirement.
    (2)   Affirmative Covenants
        Allowed in the United States, but not in England.
    (3)   Covenants to Pay Money
        Covenants to pay money for some improvement that benefits the promisor by enhancing the value of his land touches and concerns even though the improvements are on another land. (For example, annual fees for care of common areas of condos).

c . Covenant with Benefit in Gross
When the benefit of an covenant does not touch and concern land (i.e., in gross) the majority rule is that the burden will not run. What is the reason for this rule:
   (1)   English Rule
       England does not recognize an easement in gross and they consider equitable servitude to be a "negative easement" which does not run if it is in gross.
   (2)   American Rule
       America does recognize easements in gross, therefore, the burden should run. However, most courts follow the English rule. The Rationale:
       (i)   Where the burden devalues land, public policy requires an accompanying benefit to the other land;
       (ii)   Public policy disfavors covenants that do not have the purpose of dealing with externalities affecting other land;
       (iii)   Where the benefit is in gross, finding the owner to buy them out becomes more difficult than when the benefit is in the owner of neighboring land.

5 . Notice
If the assignee is a subsequent purchaser for valuable consideration without notice of the servitude, he does not take subject to it. If the assignee has notice, he is bound if the servitude is otherwise enforceable.

a . Actual Notice
If the assignee has actual knowledge of the covenant in a prior deed, he clearly has notice.

b . Record Notice
If the covenant is in a deed to the assignee's lot, he has record notice. If the covenant is in a deed or deeds to other lots in a subdivision, the assignee has record notice if the

deeds to neighboring lots are in the assignee's *chain of title*.

c. **Inquiry Notice**
At least one court has held that purchaser buying into a built-up residential area where the houses appear to have been built in accordance with a plan should look at other deeds from the developer to see if any basis for an implied covenant exists.

D. Enforcement by a Third Party or Prior Purchaser
Must distinguish between suits by *assignees* of the original promisee, who have a right to sue by virtue of stepping into the shoes of the promisee, and suits by *third party beneficiaries*.

1. **Third Party must Trace Title to Party Imposing the Covenant**
In some states, the person seeking to enforce the promise must be a grantee of the person who imposed the covenant saying that they must be in privity of estate with that party. Under this restriction, *prior purchasers in a subdivision* may be given the right to enforce restrictions imposed by the developer on lots later sold, but a person who owns the lot next door cannot enforce a covenant unless he bought the lot from the person imposing the covenant.

2. **Using Scheme to Show who has the Benefit**
If deed is silent as to who can enforce a covenant, then a prior purchaser in a subdivision can enforce the covenant if they can show that the developer had a *scheme of substantial uniformity* in land use *at the time the prior purchaser bought*, which prior purchasers relied upon in their purchase.

a. **Compare - Scheme to Imply Burden**
Even though a jurisdiction will not imply a burden from a scheme, it may *imply who has the benefit* of written covenants.

b. Developer's Right to Modify

If the developer retains the right to modify restrictions imposed on lots to be sold in the future, some cases have held that this is evidence of intent to benefit the developer personally and not the neighbors in the subdivision. The retention of this right may negate the idea of development according to a scheme.

E. Construction of Covenants

A covenant will be construed so as to carry out the intention of the parties in light of the purpose of the covenant. Some of the recurring problems are:

1. Single Family Dwelling

Covenants in residential subdivisions usually prohibit construction or maintenance of other than one single family dwelling on each lot. Problem what is a single family dwelling?

2. Whether Residential Use Only Implied

A covenant that *does not specifically* limit use of land to residential may do so inferentially by providing "no dwelling shall be built closer than 20 feet from the street or costing less that $25,000."

3. Architectural Controls

Courts hold that architectural standard committees are allowed so long as they act reasonably and in good faith.

G. Termination of Covenants and Servitudes

1. Merger

If the title to the land benefited and the title to the land burdened cone into the hands of the one person, real covenants and equitable servitudes, like easement, merge into the fee simple and cease to exist.

2 . **Equitable Defenses to Enforcement**
  a. **Estoppel**
    If a benefited party acts in such a way as to lead a reasonable person to believe that the covenant was abandoned, and the burdened party acts in reliance thereon, the benefited party may be estopped from enforcing the covenant.

  b. **Relative Hardship**
    Courts may deny an injunction when the hardship to the defendant is great and the benefit to the plaintiff is small.

  c. **Change of Conditions in Neighborhood**
    For change of neighborhood conditions to be a defense:
    (1) The change *outside* the subdivision must be so pervasive as to *make all the lots* in the subdivision unsuitable for permitted uses;
    (2) Substantial change must have occurred *within the subdivision* itself.

3 . **Eminent Domain**
  When the government by eminent domain takes title to the burdened land and condemns the covenant as well, the majority rule is that the government must pay damages to the owner of the benefited land.

XIX.   NUISANCE

A. Generally
A nuisance is an unreasonable and unprivileged interference with a person's use and substantial enjoyment of her land. Relief from nuisance was awarded at common law under the basic maxim that *one must use her property so as not to injure that of another*.

   1. Private Nuisance
   When it involves interference with the private use and enjoyment of one or more nearby properties.

   2. Public Nuisance
   When the interference is with a right common to the general public.

B. Private Nuisance

   1. Definition
   A private nuisance is conduct that causes a *substantial* interference with the private use of land and is *either*:
   (1) Intentional and unreasonable; or
   (2) Unintentional but neglect, reckless, or resulting from an abnormally dangerous activity.
   A person cannot sue claiming a private nuisance unless she has a *property interest* that is affected or alleges bodily harm as a result of the activities complained thereof.

      a. Intentional Nuisance
      The primary factor in determining an intentional nuisance is the *unreasonableness of the interference* with the neighbor's use and enjoyment. An interference is unreasonable if *the gravity of the harms outweighs the utility of the actor's conduct*.

There are several "tests" that the courts utilize:

(1) ***Gravity of Harm*** - *Restatement 2nd of Torts § 827*
The following factors must be considered in determining gravity of harm:
   (i)   Extent of harm;
   (ii) Character of harm;
   (iii) Social value of the use or enjoyment invaded;
   (iv) Suitability of the use invaded to the locality; and
   (v)   Burden on the person harmed of avoiding the harm.

(2) ***Utility of Conduct***
The following factors are to be considered in determining utility of conduct:
   (i)   Social value of the primary purpose of the conduct;
   (ii) Suitability of the conduct to the character of the locality;
   (iii) Impracticability of preventing or avoiding the invasion.

(3) ***Law and Economic Analysis***
   (i)   Who is at Fault?
   Neither A nor B is solely responsible for the cause of the harm. Both are responsible, because of the conflicting uses A and B make of their respective properties. Not a question of fault!

   (ii) ***Coase Theorem***
   Analyzes how to maximize the social value of production by putting land to its most valuable use while internalizing the cost. ***The market determines whether activity continues NOT allocated by the courts.***

110

(4) ***Jost Test***
Injured party must meet a threshold requirement showing *substantial interference before court will apply and balancing test.*

(5) *"Nuisance per se" v. "Nuisance in fact"*
Per se: an activity that is a nuisance no matter how reasonable D's conduct is (i.e., illegal activity).
In fact: an activity that is unreasonable under particular facts.

b. Unintentional Acts
An unintentional act may give rise to a nuisance when the risk of harm makes the conduct unreasonable.
"Unreasonableness" refers to whether the *actor's conduct* is negligent or reckless, along with the gravity of harm.

2. Types of Unreasonable Interferences

a. Character of the Harm
(1) Depreciation of Property Value
Use of property that depreciates the value of surrounding property is *not enough in itself* to constitute a nuisance. Even so, it is important
(2) Discomfort
Includes objectionable noise, odors, smoke and other interferences which are commonly complained. Standard of unreasonable interference is measure by the *sensibilities of the average person.* Note: Block sunlight and erecting "spite" fences which are meant to cause harm to anyone trying to enter were considered substantial interferences.

(3) Fear of Harm
If the use is a dangerous one that puts the adjoining neighbor in fear of harm, this is a

111

significant factor in declaring a nuisance. The reasonableness of the fear is tested by the *general community beliefs and extrinsic evidence* based upon experience.

   (i) Character of the Neighborhood
      Character of the neighborhood is used to determine a nuisance. Residential areas are often given preferred status and are protected against incompatible uses.

   (ii) Social Value of the Conflicting
      Primary object is to *avoid the more serious harm.* Court is more likely to enjoin conduct with less social value.

   (iii) Priority in Time
      Another important factor is which of the conflicting uses was *first located in the vicinity.* If defendant's use was first, the plaintiff has *"come to the nuisance"* and has a less appealing case because she could have avoided the harm. Although, this factor is *not always* determinative.

3 . Nuisance Compared to Trespass
A *physical invasion* of another's land can be either a trespass or a nuisance.

a. Trespass
Is an actionable invasion of a possessor's interest in exclusive *possession* of land. The plaintiff is entitled to relief upon showing of an *intentional* physical intrusion.

b. Nuisance
Is an actionable invasion of a possessor's interest in the

use and enjoyment of the land. The plaintiff must show:

   (1)   Unreasonable conduct;

(2) Substantial injury; and
(3) That the equities balance in plaintiff's favor.
Note: Air pollution can be classified as a trespass or
nuisance.

c. **Remedies**
  (1) Money damages
  (2) Injunction
  (3) Specific performance

C. Public Nuisance

1. **Definition**
  A public nuisance affects *the general public*, whereas a
  private nuisance affects only particular individuals. A public
  nuisance is widespread in its range and indiscriminate in its
  effects. The underlying test of a public nuisance is the same as
  for a private nuisance: *substantial harm* caused by an
  intentional and unreasonable conduct.

2. **Enforcement by Private Persons**
  A private individual may act against a public nuisance *only* if
  she can show that the nuisance is *specially injurious* to her.
  The person does not have to own any affected land, but she must
  show that the damage to her is of a *different kind* than
  damage to the public at large.
  The standing requirements are:
  (1) Entire community affected; and
  (2) Injury must be cognizable.

3. **Use Authorized by Statute**
  If a use is authorized by a statute or ordinance, it is not a public
  nuisance and cannot be enjoined. However, it may actionable as
  a trespass or a private nuisance.

XX. Public Land Use Controls

A. Zoning

1. Theory of Zoning
Zoning purports to prevent one land owner from harming his neighbor by brining in an incompatible use. In a sense, zoning is a nuisance law made predictable by declaring in advance what uses are harmful and prohibited in the zone.

a. Separation of Uses
Most fundamental means of achieving purposes of zoning. Highest Use → Least Harmful (i.e., housing in an industrial area). Lowest Use → Most Harmful (i.e., industry in an residential area).
  (1) Highest Use - Housing
      Zoning works on assumption that wholesome housing must be protected from harmful neighbors. The "single family home" is the highest use and is protected from commerce and industry.
  (2) Commercial and Industrial
      Commercial is lower than residential use.
      Industrial is lower that commercial and residential.
  (3) Principle of Cumulative Tests
      It states that *higher* but not lower uses are permitted in any district.

b. Density Controls
Rules that indirectly control the number of people using an area of land. They may include height limitations, setback requirements, and minimum lot and house sizes.

2. Three (3) Sources of Zoning Power
Usually enacted by a city or a county to apply to its jurisdiction. But under our government scheme, the *state legislature* is

115

the sovereign power and a city has not power to zone unless the state specifically grants that power.
Therefore:

a. **Enabling Act:** act giving power to zone from state to cities and counties.
Delegation of Power - A legislature cannot delegate discretionary authority to an administrative body unless it lays down standards to govern the exercise of power. Courts fear discretionary power because of the potential for abuse. Thus, in zoning cases where the standard to be applied *is vague* → *the delegation of authority may be challenged*. This is a very popular argument made today.

b. **Comprehensive Plan** - § 3 of the Standard Zoning Enabling Act requires that local ordinances *"be made in accordance with a comprehensive plan."* To prepare the plan, the enabling act requires that:
　　(1) Planning commission composed of citizens appointed by the mayor;
　　(2) Commission employs staff of professional planners; and
　　(3) Commission recommends ordinances to the local legislative body.
　　　　(i) Legal Effect of Plan
　　　　Plan is *a guide for development* within the city. Adoption of a plan does not restrict property use → plan must be implemented by the local legislature. Main Purpose: *Constraint on exercise of discretionary powers.*
　　　　(ii) Conflict Between Plan and Prior Ordinances
　　　　Once a plan is adopted then all preexisting ordinances *must conform.*

c. **Zoning Ordinances**
Set of regulations enacted by the local legislature and enforced by local officials.

3 . Constitutional Limitations
When a state enacts an enabling act, it does so under the authority of its police powers. However, the constitutional requirements with respect to zoning laws must be met with respect to *each individual lot*. Therefore, an ordinance may be valid in general but *invalid* as applied to a particular lot.
Arguments of Unconstitutionality Must Be Based Upon:

a **Due Process Clause of the 14**[th] **Amendment**
    (1) *Procedural Due Process*
        A landowner may argue procedural due process if the ordinance had been enacted *without notice to him and without his having an opportunity to be heard.*
        (i) Legislative Action
            Notice does not have to be given to each landowner affected.
        (ii) Administrative Action
            Notice must be given to each affected
    (2) *Substantive Due Process*
        (Note: The current Supreme Court very unlikely to extend substantive due process into this area)
        (i) Current Test
            For determining if the federal substantive due process was violated. Does the ordinance bare a *rational relationship to a permissible state objective?* (i.e., public health, safety, general welfare).
        (ii) Strict Scrutiny
            If the zoning ordinance infringes a fundamental right the burden is on the state to justify the legislation by showing a compelling state interest. Used for suspect classifications (i.e., race, national origin, alienage, gender, ethnicity, legitimacy). The most common fundamental interest is

the right of a traditional extended family to live together.

    (3)   ***State Due Process*** Requirements
State courts usually strike down "arbitrary" or "unreasonable" ordinances even though they might be a rational method.

b. Equal Protection Clause
Requires that landowners who are similarly situated be similarly treated except where treating them differently can be justified. The difference between Due Process and Equal Protection is:
    (1)   Due Process
Whether the government can take away a right?
    (2)   Equal Protection
Persons similarly situated must be similarly treated.
    (3)   For Equal Protection → discriminatory intent and purpose must be shown because discriminatory effect is not enough.

SEE LAW RULES PUBLISING CORPORATION'S EASY REVIEW CONSTITUTIONAL LAW FOR FURTHER DISCUSSION ON THIS ISSUE.

c. Takings Clause
Government cannot take away property without just compensation.

Summary of Arguments

(1) <u>Ultra Vires</u>: the action is not authorized by or violates an express provision of the enabling act.

(2) <u>Improper Delegation</u>: action is unconstitutional because the delegation of discretionary authority to the local decision maker is without government standards.

(3) <u>Procedural Due Process</u>: action (administrative decision) was taken without notice and hearing to the affected parties.

(4) <u>Substantive Due Process</u>: action deprives persons of due process because:
   a. Lack rational relationship to permissible state objective.
   b. Infringes on fundamental right and no compelling state interest.

(5) <u>Equal Protection</u>: action deprives persons of equal protection because:
   a. No rational relationship to permissible state objective.
   b. Operates by reference to suspect classification and compelling state interest.

(6) <u>Taking</u>: action takes the plaintiff's property without just compensation.

---

d. Why is Nuisance Not a Taking
Because a landowners are left with a ***reasonable return on their investment*** if they use land in compliance with zoning restrictions.

4. Purpose of Zoning

a. Zoning for Aesthetic Objectives

(1) Old Doctrine
Police power could not be used to accomplish aesthetic objectives.

(2) New Doctrine
Allow for aesthetic ordinances. ***Test: Whether the prohibited use offends the***

> *sensibilities of the average person and tends to depress property values?*

(i) Architectural Review Boards

Courts now uphold power of boards to deny permits for proposed buildings if they disapprove. Most Common Standard: Building must *"conform to the existing character of the neighborhood."*

(ii) Advertising Signs

Commercial ads can be banned in residential areas because they inhibit the area's tranquillity. However, if the sign is an expression of personal speech it cannot be banned.

b. Zoning Against Adult Entertainment

A zoning ordinance that permits adult entertainments, but disperses or limits them to certain zones, is constitutional. The biggest problem is equal protection because adult theaters are treated differently then other theaters. However, such a classification has been upheld due to unwanted secondary effects of having adult theaters in the neighborhood. *See City of Renton v. Playtime Theaters,* 475 U.S. 41, 106 S.Ct 925; *Young v. American Min. Theaters,* 475 U.S. 50, 96 S.Ct 2440.

c. Zoning for Preservation

Usually analyzed under the Takings Clause. Whether property is taken depends on analysis of the *economic loss to the landowner* weighed against the reasonable *need for legislation to accomplish a substantial public purpose.*

(1) Historic Preservation

Ordinances directed toward preservation of historical districts are generally valid. The preservation of historical districts is *not a*

120

takings violation because the landowners gains property value from the preservation.
(2) Preservation of Open Spaces
    (i) Urban Zoning
        An ordinance which prohibits the development of land is unconstitutional if the owner has no adequate return from his investment.
    (ii) Wetlands
        Usually allowed.

5. **Exclusionary Zoning**
Even where there is no INTENTION to exclude certain persons, the zoning ordinance may in fact result in exclusion.

  a. **Non-Traditional Families**
Protection of the single family home is the crux of the zoning but how do we define "single family?" Supreme Court will uphold and legislation that bears a *rational relationship* to the objective of *preserving family values*.
    (1) Excluding Group Homes for the Disabled
        Supreme Court has held that the exclusion of group homes for mentally retarded persons from areas open to those who are not retarded is a violation of the Equal Protection Clause.
    (2) Excluding Traditional Family
        A *higher standard* has been applied where the definition of family has limited the *extended family* from living together.

  b. **Low Income Persons**
Land use controls (size, acreage and value of property/house) have the effect of limiting housing for the poor.
    (1) Validity of Density Controls
        (i) Rational Relationship
            Older cases used to uphold density controls to prevent overcrowding. However, now in many states many of these laws have

been struck down because of the exclusionary effects.

    (ii) Enabling Act Violation
Many enabling acts require that cities must provide zones for all types of housing within its borders.

(2) Timing of Development
Some ordinances try to slow down housing so that the necessary public facilities (schools, hospitals) can be built to accommodate. These ordinances have the effect of discouraging newcomers to the area. The ordinances have been attacked for:

    (i) Violation of due process because not rational relationship to public welfare;

    (ii) Taking of property because some landowners will not be able to develop their property for a certain period of time.

- However most of these ordinances are *upheld if not aimed* at stopping growth of one type of housing such as low-income.

c. Racial Exclusions

Not unconstitutional because of its disproportionate impact → a racially discriminatory intent or purpose must be shown.

Factors which indicate such an intent are:
(1) Disproportionate impact;
(2) Clear pattern of discrimination;
(3) Departures from normal procedures;
(4) Statements of legislatures:

- *Fair Housing Act* - Under this act, plaintiffs only need to show that there is a discriminatory effect. A discriminatory effect is a prima facie case for a violation.

d. Federal Courts

Difficult to litigate a municipal ordinance in federal court.

Hardships of Euclidean Zoning
(1) Binds limited classes of users into tightly drawn districts.
(2) Can promote inefficient patterns of land.
(3) Can inhibit socially and aesthetically desirable diversity.

B. Achieving Flexibility in Zoning

1. Non-Conforming Uses

A non-conforming use is a *use in existence when the zoning ordinance is passed* that is not permitted in the zone in which the property is located. Non-conforming uses are permitted to remain. They may only be *limited or terminated under these conditions*:

a. Limits on Expansion and Building

Ordinance may limit expansion of the non-conforming use. May even say that once non-conforming building is destroyed it cannot be rebuilt.

b. Amortization

Ordinance may provide that the non-conforming use must *terminate after a certain reasonable period of time*. The ordinance may provide for different amortization periods depending on investment of the owner. Generally, the longer the period the more likely to be held reasonable.

(1) Majority View
Amortization is valid. Ordinances must be reasonable as applied to each non-conforming use terminated. If not, it is unconstitutional to that particular landowner.

(2) Minority View
Amortization is invalid. Some courts hold that this a taking without just compensation.

2. Amendment of Zoning Ordinance

Enabling act provides that the zoning ordinance can be amended by the local legislative body rezoning a particular parcel of land.

Local legislative body is advised by the local planning commission, but it does not have to be followed.

a. Spot Zoning
An amendment *not in accordance with the comprehensive plan.* Spot zoning is unlawful.

b. Amendments Generally Presumed Valid
Burden is on the persons objecting to the amendments. However, the trend is for courts tighten up the amendment standard.
  (1) "Change or Mistake" Rule
    This shifts the burden of proof to the proponent to show strong evidence of a mistake or substantial change in conditions.
  (2) Must Show Public Need
    Must show a public need for the change of the kind proposed.

3. Variances
Zoning enabling acts allow for the creation of the *board of adjustment to grant relief* by the way of *variance* where the restrictions contained in the ordinance cause the owner:
  (1) Practical difficulty; or
  (2) Unnecessary hardship.

a. Standards for Variances
Evidence of *practical difficulty* or *unnecessary hardship* must be strong since the variance is a departure from the uniform plan. The hardship must be due to unique circumstances peculiar to a particular lot.
  (1) The hardship cannot be self-created.
  (2) The variance must not result in detriment to public safety or welfare.

4. Special Exception
A special exception to a zoning ordinance is one allowable where certain conditions specified in the ordinance are met. Not a variance because it does not deal with undue hardship. *The*

theory is that certain uses can peacefully coexist with their neighbors when specified conditions occur. The board of adjustment is empowered to determine if a special exception exists. Problem: many times standards for special exceptions are too vague.

5 . **Discretionary or Non-Euclidean Zoning**
Under Euclidean approach the only means of flexibility provided were variances and special exceptions. These were insufficient and more flexibility was required. *Modern trend:* to uphold discretionary zoning ordinances even though may allow for favoritism or unpredictability.

    a . **Contract Zoning**
Where a city agrees to zone or rezone a particular tract of land upon the condition that the owner signs a contract restricting the use of the tract in specified ways. *Allows the owner to apply for uses that do not harm the neighbors and brings flexibility to zoning.*

    b . **Density Zoning (Cluster Zoning)**
Provides developers with an option to use spaces in various ways provided the overall density of population is maintained. For example, building several houses in corner lot and using rest of the land for a large playground.

    c . **Floating Zones**
A zone provided in the ordinance to which no land is assigned on the zoning map until a landowner makes such a request and is granted that zoning classification.

    d . **Planned Unit Development**
In a planned unit development, the developer with a large tract of land can mix uses. The developer can ignore specific lot and density requirements if the overall density does not extend the standard lot-by-lot development. Usually, a large amount of land is required.

    e . **Zoning by Referendum:** Mandatory referendums to decide zoning policies have been upheld.

XXI.   Eminent Domain

A. In General
Eminent Domain is the power the government has to take title to property against the owner's will.

Fifth (5th) Amendment states "nor shall private property be taken for public use, without just compensation." This clause has been held to be applicable to states as well as the federal government.

B.   What is a "Taking?"

1. "Taking Title"
If the government formally exercise the power of eminent domain to take title to the land then the government has taken the property and must pay fair market value for it.

2. Physical Invasion
If the government physically invades the property without taking title, it has taken the property per se and must pay for it (no matter how trivial the invasion). Physical invasion includes moving soil, water or physical bodies onto or over the plaintiff's property.

Conditional Physical Invasion
If a state regulatory action imposes a permanent physical occupation on the landowner as a condition to development of the land (such as dedication of a public easement as a condition for a building permit), the landowner can challenge the action as a taking. *See, e.g., Aris Gloves v. U.S.*, 420 F.2d 1386 (Ct. Cl.). Point here is there is no taking unless substantial disturbance of ownership rights.

3. Regulatory Taking

Example: State says owner of wetlands must not build on them. A "regulatory taking."

The regulation must bear a more compelling nexus with its objective than being merely a rational way of achieving goals.

a. Remedies Available to Landowner

Landowner may have a suit for an injunction or for damages.

(1) Suit for Injunction

A landowner may sue seeking a court to *invalidate* regulatory legislation on the grounds that it "takes" the property without just compensation.

- Many environmental laws are challenged in this fashion.

(2) Suit for Damages

Landowner may sue for damages asking, in effect, that the government pay for an interest in the property similar to a negative easement.

(3) Inverse Condemnation

A landowner is suing for compensation instead of instituting formal condemnation proceedings.

b. Tests for a Fair Taking

(1) *Harm Test*

Police Power and Eminent Domain are both subject to due process protection, the difference is this:

(i) *Eminent Domain*: Power of State to take private property for public use by government (state, municipality, federal, etc.) provided just compensation is paid. Regulation has the purpose of extracting a public benefit from the land.

Focuses on state's police power being used to prevent a harm. Just compensation is not required unless the ordinance is so onerous as to be wholly confiscatory (even in a small amount).

(ii) *Police Power*: Authoirity conferred, by the 10th Amendment to the Constitution, on the states, and delegated to local governments to ensure citizenry's safety and priviledges, public order, etc. Regulation with purpose of protecting the public from harm.

Police Power - Regulation with purpose of protecting the public from harm.

(2) *Severe Economic Loss*

Courts also look to see if there is a severe economic loss of the landowner.

Table of Cases

INDEX

A

133

C

D

E

Z